Understanding Violence

Belinda Tobin

UNDERSTANDING PRESS

Understanding Violence
Copyright © 2024 by Belinda Tobin
All rights reserved. No part of this publication may be reproduced, distributed, or transmitted in any form or by any means, including photocopying, recording, or other electronic or mechanical methods, without the prior written permission of the publisher, except in the case of brief quotations and certain other non-commercial uses permitted by copyright law.

Published by Understanding Press

UP

Paperback ISBN: 978-1-7637062-1-7
E-Book ISBN: 978-1-7637062-0-0
For permissions or enquiries, please contact:
Understanding Press
Email: up@heart-led.pub
Website: www.heart-led.pub/understanding-press
First Edition: October 2024

A catalogue record for this book is available from the National Library of Australia

Other titles in The Understanding Series:
Understanding Addiction
Understanding Sexuality
Understanding Monogamy
Understanding Creativity

I acknowledge the Yuggera and Ugarapul peoples as the Traditional Owners of the lands and waterways where this book was written. I honour the wisdom that lives within the cultures of our First Nations peoples and celebrate its continuity. I pay my deep respects to Elders past, present and future and send my greatest gratitude for all they do for the life of this land.

Always was, always will be.

An Important Note

You deserve to live a healthy and happy life.

Violence, in all its forms, is destructive. This book is here to help you understand it, not to justify or condone it or cure it.

It does not replace professional or expert advice.

So, if you or anyone you know is struggling with their own or someone else's violent behaviour, please reach out to the professional resources listed at the end of the book.

Seeking help is not a sign of weakness—it is the strongest thing you can do. Your act of bravery could be the change needed to break generations of harm.

Contents

Introduction: Understanding Violence 1

1. What Is Violence? 7
2. How Do We Know Violence Has Occurred? 23
3. Gender Differences in Violence 31
4. A Culture of Violence 43
5. Violence as a Problem-Solving Behaviour 61
6. The Beliefs Behind Violence 67
7. Violence as a Lack of Self-Control 79
8. The Emotions of Violence 85
9. The Pivotal Role of Shame and Guilt 91
10. Breaking the Cycle of Violence 105
11. The Futility of Fear-Based Approaches 115
12. Violence from a Public Health Perspective 125
13. How Economic Policy Exacerbates Violence 133
14. How the Family Court May Exacerbate Violence 141
15. Case Studies 151
16. A Personal Pathway 165
17. A Political Pathway 167

Conclusion 171

Support and Advocacy Groups 177

About the Author 179

References 181

Introduction: Understanding Violence

"Peace cannot be kept by force; it can only be achieved by understanding." – Albert Einstein.

Yet Another Crisis

This book is born out of the latest domestic violence crisis, but let's be honest—it's a crisis that's been simmering for decades. For over fifty years, successive governments have developed policies and programs aimed at preventing violence against women and children, punishing perpetrators, and supporting victims. Yet, the results have been underwhelming. This lack of progress suggests that decision-makers may not fully understand the nature of the disease they're dealing with. Or it could also be that the interventions applied need more time to take effect.

I suspect both are true. The roots of this crisis are deeply embedded in a systemic sexism that has festered for centuries. It will take sustained, dedicated effort to reverse the attitudes that are creating this tide of abuse. But I also believe that there is a simplistic and short-sighted view about the violence that is preventing effective change.

It's Not Just About "Bad People"

Much of our current approach to violence rests on the belief that it's "bad people doing bad things," as if violent individuals are somehow fundamentally different from the rest of us. This oversimplification is not only dangerous but also prevents us from fully understanding and addressing what is, in reality, a culture of violence.

The people whose actions shock us in the news may be extreme cases, but they exist within a society where various forms of violence are normalised, even celebrated. Focusing solely on those who need punishment or protection is lazy policymaking when the underlying problem continues to be perpetuated within the society in which we all live.

We Are Violent

By definition, violence involves the use of force—physical or psychological, intentional or unintentional—that results in harm or suffering.

When we take a closer look at our society, we see that many forms of violence are not only tolerated but also glorified. We cheer at tackles and punch-ups on the sports field, gamble on boxing matches, and consume endless streams of rage-bait content on social media. Our entertainment is steeped in violence, with TV shows that succeed because of bad behaviour and video games only popular because of the ability to kill and maim other characters.

Racism, bullying, and cyberbullying are also regular occurrences in our educational facilities and workplaces and, just like family violence, can have fatal consequences. There are limitless examples of workplaces that have been found guilty of breeding toxic cultures, where people live in fear and experience psychological injury. What is this, if not violence?

This issue is further complicated by the hypocrisy we see from those in authority. While political leaders may publicly denounce violence against the vulnerable, some of these same individuals engage in aggressive behaviour in parliamentary debates or support policies that cause harm, like offshore detention centres. Such behaviour from our leaders sets a troubling example and a confusing contradiction.

While addressing gendered violence is essential, we must also recognise that violence is not a male-only issue. Women and girls, too, can be violent, often in more subtle, psychological ways. Focusing solely on male-perpetrated violence is not only misguided but also dangerous.

Our younger generations are also facing an epidemic of self-harm, including cutting, purging, and binge drinking. These acts are forms of violence directed at the self. If we fail to recognise self-harm as a form of violence, we miss a crucial aspect of the problem and the bigger picture view of violence within our communities.

I Am Violent

How do we understand the violence that we see being played out across our society? Perhaps the best way is to first understand how violence plays out in our own lives.

The uncomfortable truth is that we are all capable of violence, and many of us may have already engaged in it today, even if unintentionally. This statement is not made to diminish the severity of physical assault but to emphasise that violence exists on a spectrum. In some ways, we are all complicit.

Mark Kulkens, a Clinical Psychologist who works in the field of domestic violence, once told me something that shook my world and inspired this book. He said simply,

"I am violent."

Mark was not confessing to episodic physical outbursts but rather acknowledging the many ways we can and do inflict harm on others, either intentionally or unintentionally. His words reflect a deep self-awareness and courage, and they offer powerful insight into how we, as a society, can begin to reduce the prevalence of violence by starting with ourselves.

Mahatma Gandhi captured this idea beautifully:

"We but mirror the world. All the tendencies present in the outer world are to be found in the world of our body. If we could change ourselves, the tendencies in the world would also change. As a man changes his own nature, so does the attitude of the world change towards him. We need not wait to see what others do."

Gandhi reminds us that self-awareness and individual behaviour change are crucial first steps towards creating a more peaceful society. Like Mark Kulkens, we can all play a role in understanding and taking responsibility for our actions, allowing the ripples of change to spread throughout society. However, we must also consider the context in which we operate. Change must occur at both the individual and cultural levels. If our societal mirror is cracked, it's easy to accept this brokenness as normal. But just because something is normal, it does not make it right.

Understanding Violence

As Einstein wisely said, peace cannot be imposed; it must be achieved through understanding. We must truly know what drives people to act in harmful and destructive ways. We must examine our culture and our own behaviour with honesty and courage; only then can we create effective solutions.

This book aims to help you understand violence, how to recognise it, and what drives it. My hope is that after reading it, you will be more aware of how violence manifests in your life and more equipped to take action to reduce it. With this knowledge, you can find power and become a real agent for change, both in your life and in the lives of your children.

This book also takes a holistic perspective, examining the culture in which our anti-violence policies operate, and the hypocrisies and inconsistencies in our approaches. My wish is that by doing so, we can all begin to see more clearly the inherent conflicts and contradictions in our strategies for addressing violence and work towards aligning our policies and practices for maximum effect.

UNDERSTANDING VIOLENCE

1. What Is Violence?

What do you think of when you hear the world violence? My mind immediately turns to physical brutality: a person being beaten and an accompaniment of loud, angry, hateful words. Only when I came to research this book did I realise that this is but a very extreme example of a broad spectrum of behaviours.

Firstly, though, it must be made clear that violence is a behaviour. This recognition will become more important in the coming chapters when we discuss all the contributors to making the choice to act with cruelty.

According to the United Nations, violence is a behaviour where there is an:

"Intentional or unintentional use of force or power* whether physical or psychological, threatened or actual, against an individual, oneself, or against a group of people, a community, or a government, that either results in or has a high likelihood of resulting in injury, death, psychological harm, maldevelopment or deprivation."[1]

This definition is quite lengthy and complex, so let's break it down into its components.

Intention

This definition does not discriminate against those actions taken wilfully or those occurring by accident. Therefore, violence spans the range from someone purposely punching another to a parent unexpectedly disparaging or pushing their child out of frustration. The first example involves a deliberate and perhaps even pre-meditated action. In the second, there was an unintentional reaction, a slip, a snap, and still, it can cause psychological harm.

Form

The form violence can take ranges from the physical to the psychological. That is, violence can be both seen and unseen and can be inflicted on our bodies and our minds. Examples of psychological violence include verbal aggression, coercive threats and intimidation, control, harassment or stalking, insults, humiliating and defaming conduct, as well as acts that render another person isolated from family, friends and other sources of support.[2]

Manifestation

It does not matter if the harmful behaviour is undertaken or is merely threatened; it all falls under the banner of violence. Threats create an atmosphere of fear, anxiety, and emotional distress, which can have profound psychological impacts and, therefore which can, cause significant harm.

Target

As this definition makes clear, violence can be targeted inward to oneself, outward to one another, to a group, or to complete communities. What we currently call "self-harm" fits under the category of violence, as does racism and discrimination based on belonging to any specific group of people.

Outcome

Violence can have immediate and short-term outcomes, such as an acute injury. The results can also cumulate over many years, creating chronic conditions. For example, detaining people, especially children can have horrendous effects on their physical and psychological development. Using discriminatory policies in a workplace can also deprive individuals and entire groups of the ability to provide for their families and be financially stable.

Violence Is a Vast Concept

When you think about each of these components, violence becomes an incredibly vast concept, with each event resting somewhere within the range of the following variables.

Figure 1 - The spectrum of violence

Intention	Unexpected ↔ Wilful
Form	Psychological ↔ Physical
Manifestation	Threatened ↔ Actual
Target	Self ↔ Others
Outcome	Acute ↔ Chronic

Please note that this diagram is only a very simplistic representation of all the varied ways in which violence can play out. For example, a violent act may be a single acute attack, but there can be severe psychological effects that reverberate from this one act of violence across the victim's lifetime. Similarly, while the intended target of the violence may be the self and the person may, for some time, keep the injuries a secret, when loved ones are exposed to the extent of self-harm, ripples of psychological harm pervade the person's family and friends. Nevertheless, while this model is simple, it does provide a useful tool by which we can understand just how broad and pervasive violence is.

It is Violence

The Duck Test tells us, "If it looks like a duck, swims like a duck, and quacks like a duck, then it probably is a duck". Using the definition of violence provided by the UN, we can now apply the duck test to a range of practices and become much clearer about the fact that what we are talking about is actually violence. For example:

Coercive Control

Coercive control is a pattern of behaviour in which an individual exerts power and control over another person through manipulation, intimidation, isolation, and other forms of psychological abuse. Unlike physical violence, which may be more obvious, coercive control often involves subtle, persistent tactics designed to undermine the victim's autonomy and self-worth, making it difficult for them to recognise the abuse or leave the relationship. It may include such activities as isolation, monitoring, control of resources, emotional manipulation, intimidation or degradation.

It is clear that coercive control is a behaviour that fits within the definition of violence. Whether or not it is intentional, it is a use of power against another that results in psychological injury and deprivation. Thankfully, it is increasingly recognised as a serious form of violence that can have long-lasting psychological effects on the victim. In some jurisdictions, coercive control is now being criminalised, acknowledging its harmful impact and the need for legal protection for victims.

Racism

Racism is a belief system or set of practices that discriminates against or prejudges individuals based on their race or ethnicity. It often manifests as the belief that certain races or ethnic groups are inherently superior or inferior to others, leading to unequal treatment, opportunities, and social outcomes.

Racism can occur at the individual or institutional and structural levels and include such actions as stereotyping, hate speech, discriminatory policies and procedures and economic systems that create and maintain inequality.

Any action taken, be it by an individual or by a group, that results in physical or psychological injury, maladaptation or deprivation, fulfils the definition of violence. Extrapolating this further, wherever there are racial or ethnic groups that have worse economic or health outcomes, then it is more than likely that they would be the victims of violent institutional policies. What is even sadder in this situation is racism can be internalised, leading to self-hatred or acceptance of inferior status, potentially leading to self-inflicted violence.

Discrimination

Similarly to racism, anywhere there is a person who, based on their age, gender, religion, or sexual orientation, is deprived of their ability to earn a living or participate fully in society (that is deprived), then they are also experiencing violence. The form may be predominantly psychological, but still has very real physical consequences due to the subsequent financial stress, and inability to afford housing, food and appropriate health care.

Bullying (including cyber-bullying)
Bullying is when people repeatedly and intentionally use words or actions against someone or a group of people to cause distress and risk to their wellbeing. These actions are usually done by people with more structural or social power over someone and result in the victim feeling helpless[3]. While bullying describes the type of violent behaviour being displayed, bullying is still violence. Whether it be of the physical or psychological kind, there is usually some intention to hurt another person and harm that results.

Elder Abuse
Elder abuse is a deeply concerning form of violence that targets some of the most vulnerable members of society: older adults. It encompasses various harmful actions, including physical abuse, emotional or psychological abuse, neglect, financial exploitation, and even sexual abuse. Elder abuse is particularly insidious because it often occurs in environments where seniors should feel safest, such as within their own homes, nursing facilities, or under the care of trusted family members or caregivers. The abuse can lead to severe physical injuries, emotional trauma, and financial devastation, often leaving elderly victims isolated and powerless to defend themselves or seek help. The impact of elder abuse is compounded by the victims' physical frailty, cognitive decline, and dependence on others for care, making

them less able to escape abusive situations or report their abusers.

Neglect

Neglect, particularly in the context of child or elder care, is a passive form of violence that can have devastating consequences. It involves the failure to provide necessary care, whether it be physical, emotional, or psychological, leading to significant harm to the victim. Children and the elderly are particularly vulnerable because they rely on caregivers for their basic needs, and neglect can lead to malnutrition, illness, psychological trauma, and even death. Unlike more overt forms of violence, neglect may not involve a direct action but rather a harmful omission, which can be equally destructive. The impact of neglect as a form of violence lies in its ability to deprive individuals of the care and support they need to thrive, often resulting in long-term harm and suffering.

Abusive Speech

The saying goes, "Sticks and stones can break my bones, but words will never hurt me." However, research by Dr Lisa Feldman Barrett[4] shows that chronic stress, a consequence of continued abusive speech, can weaken the immune system, cause physical illness, speed up aging and decrease lifespans. Abusive speech is that which is hateful and causes a person's sense of safety to feel threatened. Abusive speech differs from offensive speech, which is temporary, merely uncomfortable and does not have a sustained effect on your nervous system. The difference Dr Barrett explains is casual brutality versus opinions that you oppose. If something you do causes psychological stress, then it is violence. And if the behaviour continues sufficiently to cause chronic stress, then you would have also caused physical harm as well.

Self-Harm

Self-harm is more aptly named 'self-directed violence' by the United Nations because it is the use of force to cause death or physical injury. The fact that the source and the target are the same does not make it any less important to discuss and address. Because the number of people undertaking self-directed violence is substantial. In Australia alone, in 2022, 3249 people took their own lives, and 26,900 were hospitalised for self-harm injuries[5]. The actual picture of self-directed violence, though, is staggering, with a study done in 2021 finding that between the ages of 14 and 17, 30 per cent of young people (almost one in three) had thought about self-injuring, and 18 per cent (almost one in five) reported self-injury[6].

Substance Abuse

Substance abuse, including the excessive consumption of drugs, alcohol, and high-caffeine energy drinks, can be considered a form of self-harm and, therefore, a form of self-directed violence. In excess, all of these things are harmful to one's physical and mental health and can lead to a range of negative outcomes, including addiction, impaired judgment, and damage to the body and mind. Moreover, these effects ripple out to the person's friends and family, causing harm to important relationships. While substance abuse is often thought of as a cause of violence, it is less considered as an actual form of violence in itself.

Categorising substance abuse as self-harm allows us to see the extent of violence in our communities in a much more holistic light.

Sexual Harassment and Assault
Sexual harassment and assault are clear forms of violence that can be physical, emotional, and psychological. Sexual harassment involves unwanted and unwelcome behaviour of a sexual nature that creates a hostile or intimidating environment, while sexual assault refers to any non-consensual sexual contact or behaviour. Both forms of violence inflict harm by violating an individual's bodily autonomy, dignity, and sense of safety.

The trauma resulting from sexual harassment and assault can have profound and lasting effects, including PTSD, depression, anxiety, and difficulties in forming trustful relationships. These actions are not just about physical violation but also about exerting power and control over the victim, making them profoundly violent acts that can deeply scar an individual's sense of self and wellbeing.

Revenge Porn or Non-consensual Image Sharing (Including Sextortion)
Revenge porn or non-consensual image sharing involves the distribution of intimate images without the subject's consent, often with the intent to control, shame, or harm the victim. This form of violence is both sexual and psychological, as it exploits the victim's vulnerability, stripping them of their privacy and autonomy over their own body. The impact of such actions can be devastating, leading to severe emotional distress, social ostracization, and, in some cases, self-harm or

suicide. Revenge porn is a form of violence because it is a deliberate act of humiliation and control, designed to inflict maximum harm on the victim by violating their trust and exposing them to public scrutiny and judgment. This type of violence highlights the intersection of technology and abuse, where the digital dissemination of private images becomes a tool for exerting power and causing significant psychological trauma.

Incarceration

There is a growing consensus that incarceration can be considered a violent approach to justice, both in its direct effects on individuals and its broader societal implications. It involves the state's use of force to confine individuals, often under harsh and dehumanising conditions, exposing them to a risk of psychological and physical harm while in prison and poor economic and health outcomes in the longer term[7]. At the societal level, it is said that the prison system perpetuates violence, especially to marginalised groups which make up a disproportionately high level of inmates[8].

Of course, the continual justification for incarceration is that the benefit of prevention of violence to others outweighs the violence imposed on the one person jailed. Australia's recidivism rate of 42.5 per cent (returning to prison) and 51.5 per cent (returning to the criminal justice system) after two years[9] would suggest that the prisons being created to reduce violence to the community are only 50 per cent successful in the first place.

Poverty

"Poverty is the worst form of violence." ~ *Mahatma Gandhi*

Philosophers and social scientists like Johan Galtung[10] who coined the term "structural violence," argue that poverty is a form of violence because it results from unjust social arrangements that deprive individuals of achieving their potential. The harm caused by poverty is not always direct or physical, but it is pervasive and insidious, impacting individuals' wellbeing and life chances in profound ways. In this context, poverty is not just a lack of income or resources; it is a form of violence because it systematically denies people their rights and dignity, trapping them in a state of despair and suffering.

In Australia, those most likely to live in poverty are single women over sixty and Indigenous people. Poverty then is not only a form of violence in itself, but also a symptom of greater systemic violence across society. Addressing poverty, therefore, requires not just economic solutions but also a commitment to social justice and human rights, recognising that alleviating poverty is essential to reducing violence in all its forms[11].

Micro-aggression

Micro-aggression is a term introduced to describe subtle, often unintentional actions or comments that convey bias or discrimination against members of marginalised groups but which do not equate to discrimination or bullying. Unlike overt acts of racism or sexism, micro-aggressions are usually more ambiguous, making them harder to identify. Examples of micro-aggressions include derogatory remarks such as racial slurs or offensive jokes, comments that demean a person's identity, and statements or actions that negate the experiences, feelings, or realities of others.

Environmental Destruction

Environmental destruction often disproportionately affects certain communities and largely marginalised ones. It includes pollution, natural resource destruction, and practices contributing to environmental racism. These actions are considered a form of violence because they inflict harm on both individuals and communities, often leading to health issues, loss of livelihoods, and the degradation of living conditions. For example, the contamination of water supplies or the destruction of indigenous lands can result in physical illness, displacement, and cultural erasure, all of which constitute forms of violence. Environmental violence is particularly insidious because it is often systemic and perpetrated by powerful entities, leaving affected communities with little recourse or ability to protect themselves.

It's Still a Duck

The words we use matter. Whether we intend to or not, the ones we choose can disguise, distort, or obscure the true level of harm caused by these behaviours. Terms such as coercive control, incarceration, racism, discrimination, self-harm and micro-aggression are ones we come across in the news every day. We may be disturbed by them but don't necessarily see the whole picture and see them for what they are – a collection of violent behaviours. They may all be called different names, but they are still ducks.

All of these things are destructive forms of violence, yet their words don't make it obvious. For some, it may be implied, but wherever it is not evident, it requires additional levels of cognition to draw the dots between these behaviours. The implications of this are profound for individuals and policymakers.

If a person cannot see how multiple actions in their lives demonstrate or are inflicting violence, then each one is treated as a separate stressor, with potentially discounted recognition of the overall effect and application of disparate approaches.

At a governmental level, if all of these things are not seen as violence, then you can have lots of little ducks, such as the Ministers for health, justice, employment, immigration, national security, social security, women and children, communication and human rights waddling off in their own directions, creating their own terminologies and their own policies to tackle their own problems. There needs to be more consistency of understanding about the beast that they are all trying to battle. There is no combined approach, no coordination or connection, and as a result, resources are duplicated to deal with the one overall issue – that of violence. Leaders may speak passionately about separate elements of violence but do not address the overall societal issue, and therefore, sadly, opportunities for synergies are missed.

Hopefully, this chapter has given you a new perspective on the wide range of behaviours that constitute violence. Now, let's move on to understanding when we know how violence has occurred.

Core Concepts

Violence is a behaviour where there is an *intentional or unintentional use of force or power, whether physical or psychological, threatened or actual, against an individual, oneself, or against a group of people, a community, or a government, that either result in or has a high likelihood of resulting in injury, death, psychological harm, maldevelopment or deprivation.*

- Violence can be intended or inadvertent.
- Violence can by physical or psychological.
- Violence can be threatened or actual behaviour.
- Violence can deliver acute and chronic harm.

The following are actually forms of violence:
- Coercive control
- Racism
- Discrimination
- Bullying
- Elder Abuse
- Neglect
- Abusive speech
- Self-harm
- Substance abuse
- Sexual harassment and abuse
- Incarceration
- Poverty
- Revenge porn or non-consensual image sharing (including sextortion)
- Micro-aggression
- Environmental destruction.

Without a holistic view of violence, policy inconsistency and duplication of resources can occur, and opportunities for synergistic solutions missed.

UNDERSTANDING VIOLENCE

2. How Do We Know Violence Has Occurred?

"Nothing good ever comes of violence." ~ *Martin Luther*

Using the definition of violence is straightforward to determine if an act of violence has occurred. Professionals in the legal, medical, and sociological fields do this all the time to define and describe the behaviours of their clients, patients, and subjects. However, the definition presented in the previous chapter tends to focus solely on the perpetrator's actions. The reality is that violence cannot be empirically demonstrated. Its existence requires consideration of the victim's experiences and perceptions.

Violence is Subjective

There is no uniform understanding of violence across different individuals and cultural contexts. Additionally, the United Nations definition does not account for the fact that violence involves at least two parties: the offender and the victim. The victim's perception of violence can vary greatly depending on a range of factors, such as their physical and psychological state, the environment in which the incident occurs, and their past experiences (including cultural upbringing). Thus, while an action may be objectively defined as violent, it may not be perceived as such by the victim, or conversely, an action that is not typically labelled as violence might be experienced as such by someone who feels threatened or harmed by it because of their current state or past situations. Academic research, such as studies in psychology and sociology, consistently supports the notion that violence is a subjective experience shaped by individual perceptions rather than merely the actions themselves. These studies have shown that the impact of violence is often determined by how the victim experiences the behaviour rather than by the objective severity of the act[12].

Moreover, scholars have explored how cultural, social, and psychological factors influence the perception of violence. For instance, Lisa Feldman Barrett's work on emotion and perception suggests that our understanding of what constitutes violence is not hardwired but is constructed based on our previous experiences, cultural norms, and the immediate context in which an action occurs[13]. This constructionist view challenges the idea that violence is solely an objective phenomenon, highlighting the importance of the victim's perspective in defining and understanding violent acts. It is crucial to consider multiple viewpoints to fully comprehend the nature of violence.

Violence as a Form of Communication

Understanding the subjective nature of violence is helped by thinking of it as a form of communication where there is a sender (the perpetrator) and a receiver (the victim). Just like in any communicative act, the sender's intention might not always align with the receiver's interpretation. The perpetrator may intend to exert force, intimidate, or harm the victim, but how these actions are perceived can vary.

For instance, if someone shoves another person, the intent might be to assert dominance, express anger, or create physical space. However, how the receiver interprets this action can differ significantly. They might perceive it as a playful gesture, a minor annoyance, or a serious act of aggression, depending on who the sender is, where and how the event unfolds and their previous experiences with being shoved. Violence is not just an objective reality; it is also shaped by the interpretation and perception of those who experience it.

The Role of the Receiver

Three key variables influence the receiver's interpretation of violence, being[14]:

1. The receiver's physical state
2. The surroundings
3. The receiver's past experiences.

The moderation role that these things play between sender and receiver is shown in the following diagram.

Figure 2 - Variables affecting the experience of violence

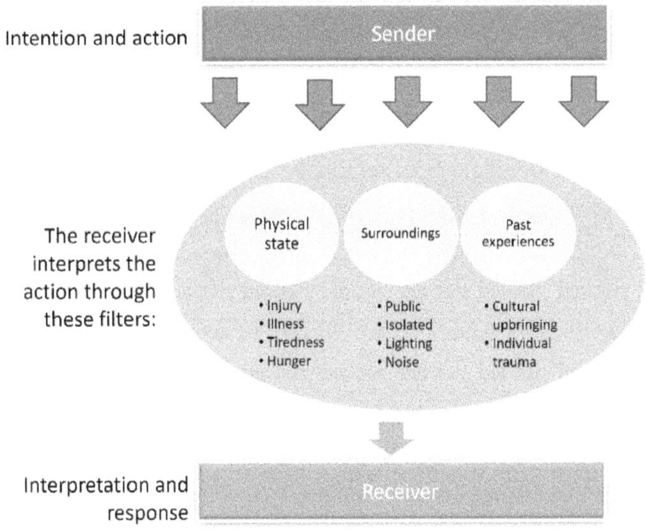

Physical State

The physical condition of the receiver can significantly influence how they perceive an action. For instance, if someone is physically vulnerable, such as being ill or injured, tired or hungry, they might perceive normally benign actions as threatening. When in a weakened physical state, the brain might interpret even minor physical contact as a potential threat, amplifying the perception of violence.

Surroundings

The environment in which an interaction occurs also plays a crucial role. A behaviour considered harmless in one context could be seen as aggressive in another. For example, a shove in a crowded sports arena might be dismissed as part of the event's excitement, while the same shove in a quiet, isolated space could be perceived as an aggressive act. The surroundings provide contextual cues that the brain uses to interpret the intentions behind an action, influencing whether it is viewed as violent.

Past Experiences

Our brains constantly draw on past experiences to make sense of the present. So, personal histories heavily inform how individuals interpret actions. Someone who has been raised in a culture where there is regular physical roughness may not regard low-level physical violence as anything other than normal. However, those who have experienced abuse in the past might be more sensitive to certain behaviours, perceiving them as violent even when others might not. The long-lasting impact of trauma on the interpretation of violence is a significant aspect to consider.

Different Views on Violence

Let's work through some more examples to further illustrate the subjective nature of violence.

Consider a scenario where an employee is given a stern reprimand by their boss in front of colleagues. According to traditional definitions, this might not be considered violent, as there is no physical harm or explicit threat. It could be dismissed as "reasonable management action". However, suppose the employee has had past experiences of bullying or verbal abuse. In that case, they might perceive this reprimand as a form of psychological violence, feeling humiliated and threatened. While others may not think it fits the requisite definition, the employee feels frightened and that they have experienced harm.

Similarly, imagine a scenario where someone playfully slaps a friend on the back. Objectively, this is a mild, non-violent action, especially in cultures where such gestures are common. However, suppose the recipient has a physical condition that makes them more sensitive to touch or has had past experiences of physical abuse. In that case, they might perceive this playful gesture as a threat. The physical pain and emotional distress caused by the slap could lead them to interpret it as a harmful act, regardless of the intent behind it.

Conversely, a person may be confronted by a gang at a fast-food restaurant, with the leader of the gang declaring, "I will kill you". Generally, this would be considered a threat and, therefore, a form of violence. However, suppose the receiver feels fit, strong, secure and supported and knows the speaker as someone who talks big in front of their people but never follows through. In that case, the impact on him may be minimal. Likewise, if this threat is delivered after a prank pulled by best friends, said in a positive, happy environment and is part of the common dialogue between the chums, then it would be dismissed readily as a joke rather than trouble.

Additionally, while we have discussed incarceration as an act of violence in the previous chapter, it may not always be seen as such by those captured in the system. For those with a high regard for authority and a belief that punishment is deserved, it may be seen as a legitimate part of a rehabilitation process. However, those who believe themselves innocent, have little trust in the justice system or have past experiences of trauma in prison, then they could easily see the act of placing them in jail as an act of harm.

There Are Two Sides to Every Story

Violence cannot be fully understood or defined solely by the perpetrator's actions. The experiences and perceptions of the victim play a critical role in determining whether an act is violent. By considering violence as a form of communication where both the sender and receiver shape the meaning, we can better appreciate the complexities involved in defining and addressing violent behaviour. The subjective nature of violence, influenced by factors such as the receiver's physical state, surroundings, and past experiences, underscores the importance of considering the victim's perspective in discussions about violence. This broader understanding can help in developing more effective interventions and support systems for those who experience violence in its many forms.

Core Concepts

The definition of violence is an objective one, but the experience of violence is subjective.

Violence is in the eye of the receiver.

Whether a person perceives that violence has been perpetrated against them depends on their:

- physical state
- surroundings
- past experiences.

The subjective nature of violence underscores the importance of considering the victim's perspective in preventative and justice policies.

3. Gender Differences in Violence

Violence is not just a male issue; women, too, must take responsibility for the violence that they perpetrate.

While it is essential to consider violence holistically, it is equally important to recognise that gender plays a critical role in shaping the forms violence takes and how it is received. Through the ages, men and women have played different societal roles, had varying expectations placed upon them, and had very disparate forms of power. Over centuries, patterns of behaviour have been formed, and through societal permission and punishment, men and women have found their unique ways to move in this world and to get what they want.

Historically, men's physical strength and dominance have been celebrated, often translating into more overt forms of physical violence. In contrast, women, who have historically been unable to compete physically, have developed other means of exerting power, such as psychological and emotional strategies, which can manifest in more subtle forms of violence. While attention must be paid to preventing physical violence, we must also acknowledge the severe impacts of the psychological and emotional violence that women have become adept at delivering.

Male Socialisation and Physical Strength

Men and boys are not just products of their parents but of cultural norms and societal expectations that have spanned generations. For centuries, men have been conditioned to use physical strength to solve problems and assert power. Physical strength and aggression are embedded within what it means for them to be masculine.

Boys are taught from a young age to be physically assertive, tough, dominant, and resilient. This is what is required to fulfil their role as protectors and providers of their families and communities. Numerous institutions, including family structures, educational systems, and the media, reinforce this process of socialisation, propagating the notion that true masculinity is synonymous with physical power.

Cultural norms celebrating male physicality are evident in the ways societies have structured gender roles. In many traditional societies, men were expected to engage in physically demanding tasks such as hunting, farming, and combat, while women were relegated to roles associated with domesticity and caregiving. This division of labour reinforced the idea that men are inherently stronger and established a gender hierarchy that positioned men as the dominant force in both the private and public spheres. Physical power also became a core part of conflict resolution, historically seen as a legitimate means of settling disputes.

"Male honour" is a concept that has been cemented within our culture and is related to the use of strength to protect a man's social standing, self-respect, family, and community. Moreover, the association of masculinity with physical power has also found its way into the corporate world, where assertiveness and competitiveness are often valued over collaboration and empathy.

The link between male physicality and dominance is further reinforced by the media, which often portrays men as strong, aggressive, and authoritative figures. From action movies to sports, men are frequently depicted as heroes who use their physical prowess to overcome obstacles and achieve their goals. These portrayals not only reflect societal values but also serve to valorise the idea that true masculinity is defined by physical strength and dominance.

One of the most influential theories in understanding male socialisation is R.W. Connell's concept of hegemonic masculinity[15]. Hegemonic masculinity refers to the culturally dominant ideal of manhood, which emphasises attributes such as toughness, stoicism, competitiveness, and the subordination of women and other marginalised groups. According to Connell, this form of masculinity is not only about physical strength but also about the social power that men wield over women and other men who do not conform to this ideal.

Connell's theory highlights how hegemonic masculinity shapes social expectations for men to be dominant and physically powerful. This expectation is internalised by many men, leading them to equate their self-worth with their ability to display strength and control. As a result, men may feel compelled to engage in behaviours that reinforce these ideals, even when such behaviours are harmful to themselves or others.

Research supports the idea that hegemonic masculinity is associated with increased aggression and violence. Studies have shown that men who strongly identify with traditional masculine norms are more likely to engage in aggressive behaviour and view violence as an acceptable means of resolving conflicts. For example, a study by Reidy et al. (2014)[16] found that adherence to masculine norms was a significant predictor of both physical and psychological aggression in intimate relationships.

Interestingly, the pressure to conform to this tough version of masculinity can cause men to suppress their emotions and vulnerabilities. Expressing feelings has often been perceived as weak or unmanly. This emotional suppression can contribute to a range of negative outcomes, including increased stress, depression, self-harm (including through substance abuse) and a higher likelihood of engaging in violent behaviour as a way to cope with these emotions. These norms around male behaviour then create both internal and external battles.

Physical force has been seen for generations as part of the value that men bring to their societies and is embedded within what it means to be a man. However, we are now witnessing how this strength can also be men's greatest weakness. How can we separate the strength from the weakness and unwind the toxic traits that have once been celebrated? It requires a massive identity shift in the understanding of what it means to be a man, and it will take many years and many helpful role models to socialise the next generations to a more positive state.

> *"Recognising that violence against women is a manifestation of historically unequal power relations between men and women, which have led to domination over and discrimination against women by men and to the prevention of the full advancement of women, and that violence against women is one of the crucial social mechanisms by which women are forced into a subordinate position compared with men."*[17]

Female Socialisation and Psychological Power

While men have historically been taught to exert physical strength, women, often unable to compete on this level due to physical and social constraints, have developed alternative means to exert power and solve conflicts. These strategies are largely psychological and emotional, allowing women to navigate social hierarchies, influence and harm others without resorting to physical force, and remain relatively hidden. They include relational aggression and emotional manipulation.

Relational Aggression

One of the primary ways women have exerted power is through relational aggression, a form of psychological violence that involves damaging another person's social relationships or status. Unlike physical aggression, which is overt and direct, relational aggression is often covert, relying on subtle manipulation, gossip, exclusion, and other social tactics to achieve its aims.

Relational aggression is really a form of subversive bullying that is particularly prevalent in female social dynamics, where relationships and social standing are often more emphasised than in male groups. Research by Crick and Grotpeter (1995)[18] found that girls are more likely than boys to engage in relational aggression, using their social networks to hurt or manipulate others. The girls use their influence, coopting their friends to isolate or psychologically injure those in the "out-group" or any other individuals who threaten them in some way.

Similarly, Ridgeway and Correll's (2004)[19] research suggests that women often use their social skills and emotional intelligence to navigate power dynamics, leveraging relationships to gain influence in both personal and professional settings. This form of aggression allows women to exert control and influence within their social circles, often without the need for direct confrontation. Relational aggression can be found frequently in the workplace, where an employee might engage in covert actions to undermine a colleague. For instance, a woman might spread rumours about a co-worker to damage their reputation or exclude them from important meetings and social gatherings to isolate them from the team.

The outcomes of this behaviour can be profoundly damaging, leading to the targeted individual feeling alienated, anxious, deprived of promotional opportunities and, due to the stress involved, less capable of performing their job. The helplessness felt by ostracised employees can have long-term effects on their mental health and professional development[20].

Increasingly relational aggression is being undertaken by females online with research showing that cyberaggression is often emitted at higher rates by females than by males.[21]

All of these outcomes of violence are achieved without the aggressor, be it girls in the schoolyard or women in the workforce, needing to resort to overt physical or verbal abuse. These forms of violence often go unnoticed by superiors, making them difficult to address.

Emotional Manipulation

Manipulation is another strategy women have employed to exert power, particularly in environments where direct action or confrontation is not possible. This can involve using charm, persuasion, persistent nagging, demeaning, deception, or verbal threats to achieve their goals and potentially harm another person.

A common example is gaslighting, where one partner might subtly manipulate the other into questioning their own perceptions or feelings. This tactic can create a power imbalance, where the manipulator gains control over the victim's thoughts and emotions and, as a result, can cause substantial psychological harm.

Women may also taunt their partner with the loss of financial resources or access to their children, which is a form of threatening behaviour, coercion and control, contributing to the cycle of violence. Statements such as "I will take you to the cleaner" suggest the speaker intends to restrain the other's financial resources or create a sense of financial dependency to manipulate and maintain power and control over the victim. Likewise, when a woman says, "I will take the kids", it plays on the victim's fears and the high stakes involved in child custody battles. These tactics are critical components of the broader spectrum of emotional abuse that victims face, and they illustrate how women use psychological and emotional forms of violence to maintain control in abusive relationships.

A woman may also use consistent comparison to create psychological harm to her partner or children. Being constantly told that they are less competent, attractive, or successful than others can lead to feelings of inadequacy and worthlessness. Over time, this can contribute to serious mental health issues, such as depression, anxiety, and low self-confidence.

Frequent interruptions or persistently nagging others over minor issues are also forms of emotional manipulation that can create a pervasive sense of frustration and anxiety. They can cause the receiver to feel perpetually on edge, creating tension and hostility. From a psychological perspective, such behaviour can be seen as a form of coercive control, where one person tries to dominate their partner's time and erode their autonomy. This tactic can diminish the partner's ability to make decisions and express themselves, leading to increased dependence and decreased personal agency.

On the other end of the spectrum, emotional neglect, especially in childhood, can lead to significant psychological injuries and developmental maladaptation. Without adequate emotional support, children may struggle to develop healthy self-esteem and might experience difficulties in forming secure attachments in their later relationships. They might also exhibit problems with emotional regulation and show increased susceptibility to anxiety and depression. In this way, a woman, who is still more than likely to be the primary caregiver for a child, can, through emotional withdrawal, cause significant psychological injury.

Cultural norms have historically celebrated women for their psychological and emotional skills. They have become experts at emotional and social manipulation because, for many years, these are the only ways that they could find some sense of control and power over their environments. Relational and emotional intelligence, like men's physicality, has been viewed as women's strength, a skill they can use to nurture, care and add value to their partners, children, colleagues and communities.

However, here we see a very similar situation occurring for women, where their strength can also become their weakness and a weapon used to wield injury. Social groups, relationships and emotional intelligence can be used as an input to violent psychological strategies. These strategies, including relational aggression, social influence, and manipulation, allow women to navigate complex social environments and exert power in ways that are often less visible but equally injurious.

Equal Rights to Perpetrate Violence

At the heart of violence is the misuse of force or power. Because men and women have different sources of power, we also see some generalisations of how they perpetrate violence. Men's power has traditionally come from physical superiority and more recently, as the "breadwinner" from control over resources. Women, though, have found their power through managing relationships and the emotional states of others. It is for these reasons we see men more likely to perpetrate physical violence and coercive control.

In contrast, girls and women tend to lean towards relational aggression and emotional manipulation to achieve their aims. It has been found time and time again that females perpetrate greater levels of verbal, and indirect, aggression than males. While the male-dominated forms of violence are the most physically injurious, the female forms can also be destructive.

Figure 3 - Sources of power and violent outcomes

	Traditional Source of Power	**How Violence Is Actualised**
Male	Physical strength Financial resources	Physical abuse Coercive control
Female	Relationships Emotional intelligence	Relational aggression Emotional manipulation

Both physical and psychological forms of violence are covered in the definition of domestic and family violence presented by Services Australia.

"Any behaviour that's violent, threatening, controlling or intended to make you or your family feel scared and unsafe can be considered family and domestic violence."[22]

The list of activities that are considered violent includes not only physical violence and sexual assault but also controlling behaviour, financial abuse, emotional abuse, stalking, and technology-facilitated abuse.

Violence is not just a male problem. It is a human problem, and we must all become aware of how we use our power to perpetrate harm. It is vital to see violence in all its forms if we are to create consistent and complementary approaches and reduce the level of aggression across society as a whole.

On an interesting note, it does appear that the equality being sought in women's rights is also playing out in the field of violence. Reports show that girls may indeed be getting more physically aggressive[23] including becoming involved in contact sports, getting into punch ups and joining violent gangs. Being physically confrontational is seen as a way to express their equality with boys. It appears that addressing toxic masculine traits is important not just for the next generations of boys and men but for our girls as well.

Core Concepts

Gendered socialisation has traditionally led men and women to have different sources of power and, thus, to display different forms of violence.

Men generally express power physically and through control of resources.

Women tend to use psychological forms of violence, including relational aggression and emotional abuse.

While physical violence receives much attention, the psychological and more subtle forms wielded by women can result in significant harm.

As women gain equality, they increasingly engage in forms of violence traditionally associated with men, including physical aggression.

4. A Culture of Violence

"Children are not born violent; they are essentially learning machines." ~ Will Linden, Scottish Violence Reduction Unit

Violence is not merely an individual issue resulting from individual pathology or isolated incidents. It can be deeply ingrained and even condoned by a society's cultural norms and values. Violence can be a pervasive part of how we live, and because of this, it becomes invisible and normalised. It becomes just part of who we are and what we do – violence becomes part of our culture. The consequence of a violent culture is that there becomes confusion about when violence is permissible and when it is not.

Where there is endorsement and legitimisation of violence to resolve conflicts, exert power, or achieve social standing in one arena, it blurs the boundaries for what is proper in others. When violent behaviour is seen daily in our media, we become desensitised and physical and psychological violence then becomes pervasive and acceptable in subtle and insidious ways.

Here are areas in which harm is displayed daily in our society and which create a culture of violence and confusion:

- Entertainment – largely through electronic media such as games, music, tv and film.
- Sport – both in front of and behind the cameras.
- Sex – through pervasive pornography.

- Politics – on the parliament floor and in government workplaces.
- News – through graphic and violent videos.
- Justice – systems and structures that excuse or enable violence.

Violence Dressed Up as Entertainment

Physical and psychological violence is widespread across all forms of electronic media. The TV shows we sit down and seek to relax to, crime dramas, action series and reality TV, regularly portray violent acts as successful tools for maintaining power and represent the perpetrators as anti-heroes. In Reality TV, participants are usually popularised based on how much drama and emotional angst they deliver to others. In shows such as The Ultimate Fighter, real-life confrontations and threats are celebrated, and participants are praised for their aggressiveness.

Online gaming has received much attention in recent years, especially First Person Shooter (FPS) games such as Fortnite, Call of Duty, Grand Theft Auto and Mortal Kombat. Here, players are rewarded for engaging in violent actions, such as killing enemies or completing missions that involve criminal activities. Mortal Kombat also glorifies extreme acts of violence with its "Fatality" moves, where characters perform gruesome finishing moves on their opponents. The violence is often stylised and exaggerated, but it is also celebrated as a key feature of the game.

Films are forms of fiction, but they also allow violent protagonists to be seen as righteous heroes who are justified in using force to overcome obstacles. The elaborate fight scenes and gun battles are a major draw for audiences, often portraying violence as thrilling.

Increasingly, music also contains lyrics that portray violence as a legitimate response, and several artists are making specific reference to sexual abuse and BDSM behaviours that bring about harm.

The age-old argument is that people understand that these sights and sounds are merely entertainment, and no one would be stupid enough to repeat them in our everyday lives. However, research shows that the electronic media that entertains us is also embedding violence. It does this mainly through the emotional stimulation that it creates. Watching, hearing or participating in harmful activities primes our brains toward aggressive concepts and transfers the excitement from the screen, song or game into our own psyche. We learn from what we see and hear and sometimes even seek to mimic it. And the more we see violence, the less it becomes concerning. With every exposure, we become desensitised. Then, we begin to seek out people who are similarly desensitised and share the same views, either in the media or in real life, therefore increasing the risk for embedded and escalated violence.

There is much compelling evidence to show that:

"Media violence increases the risk significantly that a viewer or game player will behave more violently in the short run and in the long run."[24]

This is true for both children and adults.

Moreover, the effect of media on aggressive and violent behaviour is massive. As shown in the following diagram[25], the only effect larger than the effect of media violence on aggression is that of cigarette smoking on lung cancer.

So, while we can argue that our entertainment is merely a reflection of our culture, through these means, it also facilitates the acceptance of violence on a daily basis. Art may imitate life, but it also influences it.

Figure 4 - The effect of media on aggressive and violent behaviour

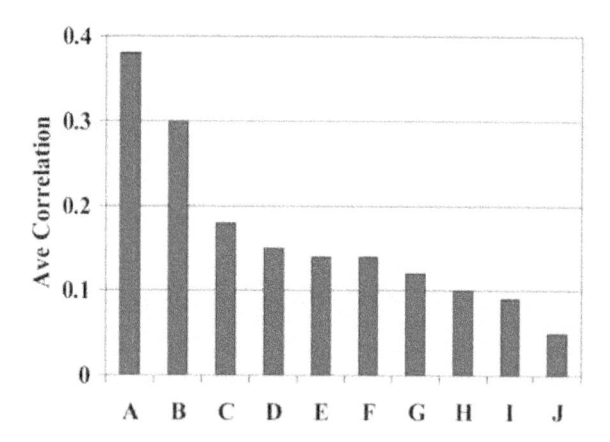

A. Smoking and lung cancer
B. Media violence and aggression
C. Condom use and sexually transmitted HIV
D. Passive smoking and lung cancer at work
E. Exposure to lead and IQ scores in children
F. Nicotine patch and smoking cessation
G. Calcium intake and bone mass
H. Homework and academic achievement
I. Exposure to asbestos and laryngeal cancer
J. Self-examination and extent of breast cancer

Violence Dressed Up as Sex

Yes, I am speaking of pornography. First, it is important to get on the same page about what we mean by pornography. The technical definition of pornography is:

"Materials produced principally for the purposes of sexual arousal."[26]

This definition sounds completely harmless; however, pornography has evolved in deeply disturbing ways:

The Normality of Violence
Nearly 90 per cent of all scenes in the top fifty porn films contained at least one aggressive act, being either physical or verbal abuse. There were, on average, twelve acts of violence per scene in these top renting films[27].

Gozo Porn
Also known as hardcore porn, depicts sexual violence, such as women being debased, dehumanised and physically tortured. Here, brutality becomes linked with sexual pleasure.

Pseudo-child pornography (PCP)
Where women are dressed like toddlers or young girls, surrounds them with childhood toys, normalising children as attractive sexual partners.

The Availability of Pornography to Children
The average teenager encounters porn at around 11 years old[28]. Most adolescents will have viewed pornography, with

around 93 per cent of boys and 62 per cent of girls regularly exposed to pornographic images[29].

Similar to the arguments dismissing violence in media, you may think any sensible person should be able to distinguish between the fantasy that porn portrays and the reality of healthy sexual relations. Unfortunately, you would be wrong. Around 44 per cent of males and 29 per cent of females report wanting to act out what they see in porn[30]. Three-quarters of young women say that pornography increases pressure on girls to act a certain way and increases their level of insecurity in intimate relationships[31]. Around 70 per cent of teenage boys admit that pornography has had a damaging impact on their view of sex and relationships[32].

Porn, it seems, is today's source of sex education with severe and negative consequences. Research reveals that this consumption strengthens harmful gender stereotypes and increases the perpetration of sexual aggression and tolerance of receiving it. It fills our children's minds with lies about sexual relations. For example, it creates the impression that women are always up for sex and are always willing to do what a man wants, regardless of how painful, harmful or humiliating it may be[33]. While parents and educators may desire to create an environment of gender equality and respect, porn is much louder than the positive messages. We all know that it is generally the loudest voice that wins.

The research also shows that exposure to violent porn quickly escalates viewing preferences to even more violent and bizarre sexual practices. Alarmingly, the research also shows that PCP increases the demand for real child pornography and provides men with both a blueprint and stimulus to undertaking child sexual abuse[34].

Violence Dressed Up as Sport

One of the most confronting statistics I have come across when researching this book was this:

Domestic violence rates increased by 40.7 per cent on State of Origin nights[35].

The University of Lancaster in 2014 also found that family violence increased 38 per cent when England lost the World Cup and rose 26 per cent when England won or drew[36]. Similar studies in the USA showed a clear link between major sporting events and an increase in domestic violence rates.

Why? Why do games meant to bring so much pleasure to the audience end up causing so much pain? It is because there is a normalisation of male aggression and violence within sport, and sometimes even a glorification of it. Similarly to the violence we see perpetrated on TV and in games, it primes our brains for aggression. It excites us enough emotionally to reduce our natural inhibitions.

The crowd cheers when there is a punch-up on the field. And it is all over the news headlines and social media the next day. Even if there is no fight, the up-in-your-face aggression, the threats and intimidation are all seen as part of the excitement. It is not called violence but excused as someone losing their cool in the heat of the moment and an inherent part of a high-pressure game. While there are increasing penalties for those players who undertake harmful activity, suspensions and fines are slaps on the wrist compared to how these people would be punished if they undertook the same behaviour on the streets.

However, what we see on the sporting field is just one part of the picture. Physical and psychological violence has become inculcated within all sporting practices. It does not matter whether a person is involved in individual or team sport, whether they are in competitive or recreational contexts; violence perpetrated by teammates, parents, coaches and spectators is common.

Research has found that over half of teenagers (52 per cent) report being exposed to psychological violence by teammates, coaches, and parents, with ten per cent being the victim of both physical and psychological violence undertaken by various perpetrators[37].

Interestingly, while the media portrays the male coach as the most likely to be violent, the research has found that the most prevalent perpetrators are male peer athletes. Violence by spectators may be seen as rare, but when you consider the psychological harm done by slurs hurled at players, it is likely far more prevalent than first thought.

The masculine socialisation myths are embedded into sport; you have to be tough, and to be tough, you have to receive tough treatment. In fact, the opposite holds true. Teenagers exposed to interpersonal violence in their sporting pursuits can present mental health issues such as PTSD, anxiety, depression, and social isolation and undertake various forms of self-harm (self-injury, disordered eating, and suicide attempts), perpetrating the violence inwards.

Many people's sporting idols and peers shape a significant sense of identity. They seek to emulate these people, who they view as strong and successful. So, when sportspeople undertake violent behaviour, they become dangerous role models and sustain a harmful standard about how violence can be used to solve problems. Moreover, when there is little consequence for violence perpetrated by coaches, spectators or parents, then harm becomes part and parcel of the sporting culture, influencing not only those who participate in it but those who watch it as well.

Violence Dressed Up as Politics

Only last week, the news headlines were full of reports about a federal politician being heckled and hit with a wall of noise from those opposite. Their aim was to not let her be heard, for her views contradicted their sensibilities. This event comes after reports illustrating the prevalence of bullying in parliamentary workplaces and regular occurrences of insults to gain a political edge. Some may say that this is just the expected rough and tumble of politics, that is a tough game that you have to play hard. This response, however, is further evidence of how normalised violence has become in political discourse[38].

In Australian parliaments, there may not be the physical outbursts that occur elsewhere in the world. However, verbal aggression is accepted, sometimes condoned, and sometimes even encouraged. Moreover, aggressive rhetoric, derogatory language, intimidation, and emotional manipulation are often seen as legitimate strategies for political gain: to dominate debates, silence opposition, or undermine the credibility of other politicians[39].

The research has shown that the ongoing use of verbal abuse not only creates a hostile work environment but has a direct effect on the mental health of the target[40]. We have also heard that over time, psychological stress can have physical consequences, making government a very dangerous work environment indeed.

In addition to the direct harm that psychological violence does to the receivers in our governments, there are other catastrophic consequences:

- There is less likely to be support for anti-violence policies when presented by people who perpetrate violence in their workplace and public spheres.
- It raises questions about the effectiveness of those policies when developed by someone who is not really committed to change.
- It acts to normalise violence more broadly.
- It dissuades potentially great political candidates from entering government, and in this way, democracy loses out.

It is clear that, given the paternalistic histories of our parliaments, many of the destructive elements of masculine socialisation have become established. It will take a lot of introspection and courageous role-modelling by our politicians to present an alternative to solving problems with aggression and gaining political gain by harming others.

Violence Dressed Up as News

There is a very disturbing saying in journalism – that "if it bleeds, it leads." Media outlets know that sensational headlines and gory stories sell. However, graphic images of death and destruction (called traumatic media) are harmful, and the publishing of them can be seen to meet the definition of violence. Media companies intentionally use their power of publication to put out material highly likely to do psychological harm.

What is more worrying is that the top executives of firms such as Meta have been well aware of the harm being caused, especially to young people, but failed to take action to protect them. Violence sells, and profit is more important than their user's safety.

All news services make daily decisions about what should be shown in the public interest. Still, unfortunately, many cross the line and cover harmful, violent content with the façade of news. While they are attracting followers and winning the ratings wars, they are also putting their viewers at risk of media-induced trauma that can have severe mental and physical effects[41]. So, not only is the material they are publishing violent, but in doing so, they are also perpetrating violence upon the people they claim to serve.

There is an additional consequence of the proliferation and consumption of traumatic media. That is the desensitisation that occurs when we are constantly exposed to horrific scenes of crime, collisions, wars, disasters, disease and desperation. When we are no longer shocked by these things, stirring empathy is much more difficult[42]. The violence we see around us is commonplace, and then we are less likely to take action to address it. Violence becomes part of our everyday reality, and we begin to take it for granted.

Violence Dressed Up as Justice

Research indicates that violence is deeply ingrained in various aspects of the justice system, particularly through systemic practices that embed harm and inequality. For instance, systemic racism within law enforcement and criminal justice institutions perpetuates violence against marginalised communities. This systemic violence is not limited to physical acts but also includes psychological harm and the denial of justice, which reinforces the cycle of violence and oppression. Practices such as solitary confinement are also forms of psychological violence, with the likelihood of severe mental health impacts, including depression, anxiety, and hallucinations.

Moreover, studies have shown that the overuse of incarceration and punitive measures disproportionately affects vulnerable populations, leading to further entrenchment of violence within these communities. The justice system's reliance on harsh penalties and aggressive policing tactics often results in a cycle of violence that is difficult to break, perpetuating harm rather than fostering rehabilitation or justice.

The psychological impact on those working within the justice system, such as law enforcement officers, further compounds this issue. Officers often experience mental health challenges due to the violent and high-stress nature of their work, which can lead to aggressive behaviour and the normalisation of violence as a tool for maintaining order.

On the flip side, the minimising of psychological violence in legal proceedings also works to quietly condone and normalise this type of violence. Studies have shown that despite the severe and long-lasting impacts of psychological violence, it is frequently underreported and underprosecuted. Societal norms that do not recognise non-physical forms of abuse as "real" violence play a large role in this situation.

Legal systems frequently prioritise physical violence, while psychological and emotional abuses are harder to prove, leading to these forms of violence being downplayed in legal proceedings. The consequence is that the full picture of violence and the perpetration of it across the parties is not fully appreciated. Whereas those perpetrating physical violence are punished, those undertaking psychological harm may not be held to account, resulting in minimal legal recourse for victims[43]. Given that it is most frequently men who undertake physical violence and women who work with psychological harm, the overall outcome may be an imbalance in accountability for violence across the justice system.

We see the same situation occurring in the workplace, where physical injuries are readily approved in the worker's compensation system, but psychological injury approvals are drastically low. It appears that there is both a difficulty in assessing objectively the results of subjective experience and an unwillingness to hold those in power accountable for the harmful environments that they impose on their people.

One of the greatest examples of how violence can be dressed up as justice is when we see the ongoing deaths of First Nations Peoples in police custody, with over 437 such deaths reported since the 1991 Royal Commission into Aboriginal Deaths in Custody. Despite numerous recommendations from the commission, systemic issues remain largely unaddressed, contributing to continued violence against Aboriginal people by law enforcement. The high rates of imprisonment and violence faced by these communities reflect broader systemic inequalities and have led to calls for significant reforms within the Australian justice system.

Violence Dressed Up as National Security

In Australia, the concept of national security has also been used to justify actions that can be considered forms of state-sanctioned violence. Here are a few examples of how this plays out.

Anti-Terrorism Legislation and Indefinite Detention

Australia has passed a series of anti-terrorism laws that give the government broad powers to detain individuals without charge, sometimes indefinitely. The most notable example is the legislation that allows for "preventive detention orders" and "control orders." These laws permit the detention of individuals suspected of involvement in terrorism without the standard legal process, including a fair trial. Critics argue that such measures can lead to psychological harm, erode civil rights and promote a culture of fear and control.

Immigration Detention

Australia's offshore detention centres, particularly those on Manus Island and Nauru, have been criticised for their harsh conditions and the use of excessive force by security personnel. These centres are part of Australia's immigration policy aimed at deterring asylum seekers arriving by boat, often justified under the banner of national security. Reports of physical violence, abuse, and psychological trauma within these centres are widespread. Detainees, including children, have been subjected to inhumane conditions, and the use of force by security personnel has been documented as a method of maintaining order, often resulting in harm to detainees. Organisations like Amnesty International and the United Nations have condemned Australia's treatment of asylum seekers, arguing that these practices amount to state-sanctioned violence under the guise of border protection.

Surveillance and Policing Powers

Australia has enacted laws that expand government surveillance capabilities, including the mandatory data retention scheme. Under these laws, government agencies can collect and store vast amounts of data on Australian citizens without a warrant, justified as necessary for national security. The extensive surveillance powers can be seen as a form of psychological violence, as they create a pervasive sense of being watched, which can stifle free expression and dissent. The fear of surveillance and potential repercussions can have a chilling effect on political activism and public discourse. The Australian Human Rights Commission and other civil society groups have raised concerns about the impact of these laws on privacy and civil liberties.

Suppression of Dissent

In recent years, there have been instances where the Australian government has used national security as a justification to crack down on protests and public dissent. For example, laws have been enacted that criminalise certain forms of protest, particularly those related to environmental activism. There have been reports of heavy-handed policing at protests, including the use of excessive force and mass arrests. These actions are often justified as necessary to maintain public order and national security but can be seen as a form of state violence against citizens exercising their democratic rights. The International Network of Civil Liberties Organizations (INCLO) and Human Rights Watch have documented instances where Australian police have used disproportionate force against protesters, raising concerns about the suppression of dissent under the guise of national security.

These examples illustrate how the concept of national security can and is being used in Australia to justify actions that may infringe on individual rights and freedoms. These practices often lead to violence or coercive state control, which has sparked significant debate and criticism from human rights organisations and civil liberties advocates.

Adapting to an Environment of Aggression

The boundaries between entertainment, sport, politics, news, and justice are increasingly blurred by the pervasive presence of violence. We might excuse these manifestations by claiming, "It is not violence, it is just entertainment," or by rationalising brutality as inherent to sport, politics, or even justice. Yet, these daily encounters with violence subtly shape our behaviours, teaching us that aggression is not only permissible but, in some cases, desirable—whether on the playing field, in the bedroom, or in the corridors of power.

This normalisation of violence seeps into every facet of our lives, creating a society where aggression is seen as a valid means to achieve pleasure, exert power, or resolve conflict. The pervasive nature of this culture means that if we are to make genuine strides toward reducing violence, we must adopt a clear, consistent stance against all forms of aggression. As Albert Einstein noted,

"Confusion of goals and perfection of means seems, in my opinion, to characterise our age."

When the lines between acceptable and unacceptable violence are blurred, it allows for a dangerous creep of aggressive behaviour into areas where it should never be tolerated.

People inevitably adapt to their environments. As long as violence remains woven into the fabric of our culture, we will become increasingly desensitised and more willing to accept it as a normal part of life. The battles we face to prevent violence will only grow more challenging as this desensitisation takes root. To combat this, we must recognise that reducing violence in any one area requires a commitment to addressing it in all areas, ensuring that our society no longer teaches us that violence is an acceptable solution to our problems.

Core Concepts

Violence has become embedded in our culture.

The use of violence to resolve conflicts, exert power, or achieve social standing in one arena blurs the boundaries for what is proper in others.

Violence is dressed up in many ways in our culture, including in:

- Entertainment
- Pornography
- Sport
- Politics
- News
- National security
- Justice.

Media violence increases the risk significantly that a viewer or game player will behave more violently in the short run and in the long run.

Porn is today's source of sex education with severe and negative consequences. Research reveals porn strengthens harmful gender stereotypes and increases the perpetration of sexual aggression and tolerance of receiving it.

Aggression and violence have become normalised in sport, both on and off the field.

Derogatory language, abusive rhetoric, intimidation, and emotional manipulation are often seen as legitimate strategies for political gain but are violence dressed up as politics.

Media publish violent and traumatic images under the guise of news, which can cause long-term detrimental effects to the viewers.

Violence is deeply ingrained in various aspects of the justice system, particularly through systemic practices that perpetuate harm and inequality.

In Australia, the concept of national security has been used to justify actions that can be considered forms of state-sanctioned violence with a key example being immigration detention.

People become desensitised to the violence that they see, making interventions and treatments more difficult.

Reducing violence requires a dedicated and consistent commitment to addressing it in all areas.

5. Violence as a Problem-Solving Behaviour

While violence can be manifest in gangs and groups, it is fundamentally an individual behaviour. More specifically, it can be understood as a problem-solving behaviour that people may resort to when other avenues of resolution seem unavailable or ineffective. The lack of alternatives to violence can stem from:

1. Not having an awareness of or capability in other techniques that could be effective (not having alternative capacity).
2. Trying other strategies in the past which have continually proved to be unsuccessful (not having alternative confidence).

The problems that people seek to solve with violence are vast and varied but can be whittled down to a combination of:
- What they are seeking to gain and
- What they are seeking to get rid of.

They seek to gain resources, power, control, or compliance from others or they seek to remove conflict, frustration, or a perceived threat.

The key point is that violence is seldom perpetrated just for pleasure. While sadism does exist, it is rare. Research shows that only around five to six per cent of violent men are violent because they enjoy the pain they cause[44]. For most people, there is an inbuilt repulsion towards violence and inflicting pain. However, repeated exposure can make violent behaviour a habit. Like any addiction, it can escalate in both severity and quantity over time. Nevertheless, the majority of those that we would class as sadists began their foray into violence to solve a problem.

Thanks to extensive research in psychology and sociology, we now understand a person's internal process before undertaking harmful and destructive behaviours. The Cognitive Behavioural Therapy Model (CBTM) shows this cycle of decision-making.

Figure 5 - The Cognitive Behavioural Therapy Model

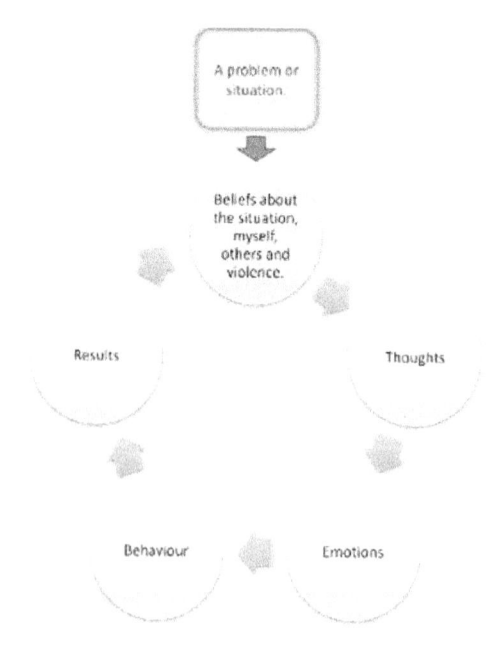

A problem or situation.

⬇

Beliefs about the situation, myself, others and violence.

Results

Thoughts

Behaviour

Emotions

Let's see how this process plays out in two very different situations.

Example 1 – Encountering a snake on a bush walk	
Beliefs	The snake is out to hurt me. I am under threat. Violence is justified for self-protection
Thoughts	I will kill the snake
Emotions	Fear Anger Aggression
Behaviour	The person throws a rock at it.
Results	The snake dies.
Influence on Beliefs	Violence is an effective way of reducing a threat.

Example 2 – A person with opposing views stands to speak in parliament	
Beliefs	The other person is out to undermine me. I am under threat. I deserve respect. Stopping her speaking is justified to protect my pride.
Thoughts	I will not let the person speak.
Emotions	Fear Anger Aggression
Behaviour	The person heckles the other so that they cannot be heard.
Results	The other sits down, frustrated and does not speak.
Influence on Beliefs	Violence is an effective way of reducing a threat.

These scenarios play out in very different settings, yet some common behaviours exist in each. The first is the perpetrator's beliefs, specifically that they were under threat and that violence was a justifiable action in the situation. The second is the lack of personal restraint shown to stop the emotions of fear and anger being manifest in action.

In the following sections, we look more closely at these two critical elements of the cycle of violence:
1. The beliefs that people hold about the situation they face, themselves, others, and about violence.
2. The moderating factors that can encourage or interrupt the progression of aggressive emotions to violent behaviour.

Core Concepts

Violence is ultimately an individual behaviour.

Violence is predominantly undertaken to achieve a goal or solve a problem for example:

- To gain resources, power, control, or compliance from others or
- To remove conflict, frustration, or a perceived threat.

People may not have options to violent reactions due to:

- Lack of awareness or capability in alternative behaviours (alternative capacity).
- Lack of faith in the effectiveness of more peaceful means (alternative confidence).

There are two key elements of the behaviour cycle where interventions can be incredibly effective:

- Beliefs – changing how people perceive the situation, themselves or violence.
- Between emotions and behaviour – enhancing a person's ability to use self-restraint.

Reducing violence requires a dedicated and consistent commitment to addressing it in all areas.

6. The Beliefs Behind Violence

"The outer conditions of a person's life will always be found to reflect their inner beliefs." ~ James Allen

You may have heard the saying that beliefs shape our reality. It is true in every area of our lives, including our experience with violence. What we hold as truths—about ourselves, our situations, and about violence—plays a crucial role in determining our behaviour. In this chapter, we will explore the intricate web of beliefs that drive individuals toward violence or make them feel as though they are on the receiving end of it. These beliefs are central to understanding why violence occurs and how it might be prevented.

Beliefs About the Situation – I Am Under Threat

Our beliefs about the situations we face are foundational in determining our responses. For example, what is your initial reaction when you see a snake crossing your path? If you perceive a situation as threatening, whether physically or psychologically, you are more likely to resort to violence, either as a pre-emptive strike or a means of self-defence. This perception of threat is often influenced by the belief that "the other" is seeking to harm you and cannot be trusted.

For instance, perpetrators of violence often view themselves as under attack by their victims, a belief that justifies their aggressive actions. This belief is not just a rationalisation but a deeply ingrained perspective that shapes how they interpret the behaviour of others. When one believes they are under threat, that they are vulnerable to physical or psychological injury, the automatic response can be to counteract that threat with violence. In this way we are no different to an animal being cornered by a potential predator. They will fight to get out and to be free. When humans also feel vulnerable, they are likely to lash out to protect themselves and escape.

The research undertaken by Dr Lisa Feldman Barrett shows that our brains are predictive tools[45], using signs and signals around us and our own personal history to decide whether we are vulnerable. The factors that come into play in shaping our view of the situation include:

Figure 6 – Factors that influence our view of the situation

Physical Sensations + Surrounding Environment + Past Experiences

Physical Sensations
Such as being tired, hungry, or anxious—can heighten an individual's feelings of vulnerability and perception of threat, making them more likely to respond violently.

The Surrounding Environment
Individuals who feel isolated or unsupported are more likely to perceive situations as threatening and resort to violence as a means of self-defence.

Past Experiences

Previous violence from the other person, or similar scenarios that were hurtful in the past can lead one to assume that the same results will occur in this new situation, and shape a person's view of the other's behaviour.

Beliefs About Ourselves – I Am Right and Deserve Respect

Our self-concept is another powerful determinant of violent behaviour. People who believe that they are inherently right and that others are wrong—often driven by a sense of moral idealism—are particularly prone to committing violence. This belief is deeply disturbing and tragic because it drives individuals to commit atrocities under the guise of doing good. Moral idealism can lead to what psychologists call "righteous violence," where the perpetrator feels morally justified in using violence to achieve what they see as a noble goal. This type of violence is often seen in both political and religious contexts, where the ends are believed to justify the means. Throughout history, some of the worst acts of violence have been perpetrated by those who genuinely believed they were acting in the service of a higher cause. Colonialism is a cruel case in point.

On a more personal level, individuals with inflated self-esteem (also known as narcissists) are also more likely to engage in violence, especially when their self-image is threatened. Here, individuals have fragile egos and may use physical or psychological means to address criticism or perceived slights to defend their vulnerable sense of self. Research by Baumeister[46] has shown that people with high but unstable favourable views of themselves often choose violence as a response to perceived threats to their pride.

"Violence ensues when people feel that their favourable views of themselves are threatened or disputed by others. As a result, people whose self-esteem is high but lacks a firm basis in genuine accomplishment are especially prone to be violent because they are most likely to have their narcissistic bubble burst." ~ Roy F. Baumeister

---

It has been shown that narcissism is related to all forms of aggression (i.e., indirect, direct, displaced, physical, verbal, bullying) and both functions of aggression (i.e., reactive, proactive). The relation between narcissism and aggression was significant for males and females, for people of all ages, for students and nonstudents, and for people from individualistic and collectivistic countries. It does not always require provocation for the aggression to manifest, for it has also been found that individuals high in narcissism have "thin skins", with it taking little stirring for violent responses to be seen as justified[47].

The belief—that one is superior and, therefore, deserves special treatment—can lead to a sense of entitlement, where violence is seen as a justified response to any challenge or disrespect. This belief is not only true on an individual level but also on a collective one, where nations or groups with inflated senses of superiority may resort to violence to assert their dominance, command the respect they believe they deserve, or avenge perceived wrongs.

Beliefs About Violence – This Is Not Violence

Being labelled as a perpetrator of violence is a badge that many people do not want to wear. As we will discuss later, it comes with much shame and guilt and goes against the people we seek to be. However, what if we believed what we were doing was not actually violence?

People may not always perceive certain behaviours as violent, particularly when the effects of those behaviours are not immediately visible or fully understood. For instance, psychological violence—such as manipulation, gaslighting, or emotional abuse—is often not recognised as violence because it lacks the physical markers that typically define violent acts. Such is true in cases where the perpetrator does not intend to cause harm or believes their actions are justified, such as making derogatory remarks or engaging in persistent criticism under the guise of concern or humour.

Similarly, physical taunts or minor acts of aggression, like pushing or teasing, may not be seen as violent by the perpetrator if they do not intend to harm the other person. However, as we have seen in the definition of violence, the harm can be unintentional. The receiver might experience these actions as deeply hurtful, leading to emotional or psychological distress. This disparity in perception is often due to a lack of understanding of the broader impacts of such behaviours, where the damage is internal and not as easily recognised or acknowledged as traditional forms of violence. Another prime example is self-harm, which is not always seen as violence against the self. This gap in perception underscores the importance of educating people about the full spectrum of violence, including its psychological forms, and acknowledging that harm can be both physical and emotional, intentional or unintentional.

Beliefs About Violence – It Works and is Justified

Beliefs about the effectiveness and legitimacy of violence are perhaps the most direct drivers of violent behaviour. Many individuals believe that violence works, at least in the short term, to achieve their goals—whether those goals are to gain power, control, or material wealth. This belief is reinforced by societal and cultural norms that sometimes glorify violent behaviour to resolve conflicts or to assert one's will. All of the examples of violence discussed in the previous chapter that are embedded into our culture help to normalise violence and create the seed of speculation in a person's mind that perhaps violence could be a legitimate and justifiable tool in this situation.

Of course, there are many other factors that go into shaping the belief that violence is acceptable. A range of factors, including genetics, gender, and cultural history, influence the belief that violence is justified or even legitimate in certain situations. In some cultures, particularly those with strong honour traditions, violence is not only accepted but expected as a means of defending one's reputation or family. These cultural norms can be deeply embedded, with violent behavioural responses passed down through generations.

However, while violence may seem effective in the short term, it often leads to greater issues in the long run. For instance, criminals may successfully use violence to acquire money or other valuables. Nevertheless, the long-term consequences often include increased insecurity, a perpetual state of threat, and the possibility of retaliation. Violence as a problem-solving tool is inherently flawed because it tends to perpetuate the very issues it seeks to resolve, leading to cycles of aggression and retribution.

"Violence is a poor means to acquire material wealth and sustain power, but it can create short-term power and dominance in interpersonal relationships." ~ Roy F. Baumeister

The surroundings and past experiences highlighted by Barrett as a predictive tool also play a role in shaping the belief that violence is right and just. Suppose a person is amongst a peer group for which violent behaviour is not only acceptable but celebrated as a badge of honour. In that case, it will influence the person's belief that violence is a legitimate action. Similarly, if a person has used violence as a problem-solving tool in the past, and it worked, they would be primed and ready to try it again. Repetition of violence is even more likely if there were few or unimportant consequences as a result of their previous behaviour.

The lack of awareness or belief in alternatives to violence is also a significant factor in the perpetuation of violent behaviour. Many individuals, especially those raised in environments where violence is prevalent, may not know any other way to resolve conflicts. Social Learning Theory explains how individuals may observe violence being used successfully as a problem-solving strategy in their environment—whether in the family, community, or media—and consequently adopt it as a viable approach to dealing with their own problems. This theory highlights how violence can become embedded within societies where it is modelled and rewarded, reinforcing its use as a problem-solving tool.

Beliefs About the Alternatives to Violence – They Don't Work

When peaceful means of conflict resolution are perceived as ineffective, individuals are likelier to turn to violence as an alternative. This belief is often reinforced in environments where systemic and structural violence—such as discrimination, racism, and inequality—are prevalent, leading to frustration and a sense of helplessness. In such cases, violence becomes a direct, albeit destructive, method of addressing perceived wrongs or achieving desired outcomes when other strategies are inaccessible or have failed[48]. In such contexts, individuals may feel that violence is the only option left to them, leading to a cycle of aggression that is difficult to break. The added implication is that it creates an environment of hypocrisy, where violence is used to address violence, legitimising this form of problem-solving even further.

Changing Beliefs

"If you don't change your beliefs, your life will be like this forever. Is that good news?" ~ W. Somerset Maugham

The tables on the following page examine how changing our beliefs can disrupt the cycle of violence and lead to other actions. They show the powerful roles that beliefs play in our conducting and experiencing violence. Changes in the way we perceive the situation, ourselves and our entitlements, and what constitutes violence can have a dramatic effect on whether we then go on to choose harmful behaviours. Therefore, if we can shift the way people see violence, then we have a chance to prevent it.

Example 1 – Encountering a snake on a bush walk		
	Old	New
Beliefs	The snake is out to hurt me. I am under threat. Violence is justified for self-protection	The snake is not out to hurt me. I am not under threat. It will go away if I let it.
Thoughts	I will kill the snake	I will remain calm and still.
Emotions	Fear Anger Aggression	Fear
Behaviour	The person throws a rock at it.	The person stands still and the snake slithers away.
Results	The snake dies.	Both the snake and person continue in peace.
Influence on Beliefs	Violence is an effective way of reducing a threat.	Leaving snakes alone is an effective means of reducing the threat.

UNDERSTANDING VIOLENCE

Example 2 – A person with opposing views stands to speak		
	Old	New
Beliefs	The other person is out to undermine me. I am under threat. Stopping her speaking is justified for protection of my pride.	My opinions are about to be challenged. I deserve respect but so does the other person.
Thoughts	I will not let the person speak.	This will be hard to hear but I will let her speak.
Emotions	Fear Anger Aggression	Fear.
Behaviour	The person heckles the other so that they cannot be heard.	The person sits in an uncomfortable silence.
Results	The other sits down, frustrated and does not speak.	The other sits down feeling heard. The person feels stronger for being able to hear alternate views.
Influence on Beliefs	Violence is an effective way of reducing a threat.	Choosing non-violent action increased my sense of strength and influence.

Core Concepts

What we believe becomes our reality.

When we believe we are in a situation of threat, we are more likely to respond with violent behaviours.

Most perpetrators of violence feel that they are under threat in some way.

Physical state, the surrounding environment and past experiences can influence perceptions of vulnerability.

Those with an inflated and yet unstable sense of self-esteem tend to use violence to prevent and address criticism.

People's beliefs about violence also influence the actions that they take, including whether they see the solution as violence and whether, in this case, it is justified.

The cultural context teaches people that some forms of violence are legitimate to solve problems.

Where people have perpetrated violence in the past with no consequence, this bolsters their belief in its efficacy and their right to respond in harmful ways.

Where there is structural and systematic violence, such as racism, discrimination and inequality, and previous peaceful means have been ineffective, violence may seem to be the only available solution.

7. Violence as a Lack of Self-Control

Let's be honest. We all have violent thoughts. Others might hurt us so badly or frustrate us so severely that we may go through periods of honestly wishing them harm. We must be clear though, this does not make us bad people. It makes us human. Our brains are wired to get out of situations that threaten our safety, so we will scan through all available options to reduce stress. But we are not our thoughts. Neither are we, our emotions. We all feel fear, we all desire to feel powerful and in control, and we all get angry. Again, feeling these things is not the issue. It is what we do with them that counts.

What is clear in the CBTM is that while emotions may drive behaviour, there is a gap between them. We may feel angry, but that does not mean we have to act on it. The concept of our ability to choose our responses to any situation is beautifully described by Viktor Frankl.

"Between stimulus and response there is a space. In that space is our power to choose our response. In our response lies our growth and our freedom." ~ Viktor Frankl.

The space between stimulus and response is where we have the opportunity to enact self-control and choose alternatives to violence. In this way, violent behaviour can be prevented by self-control.

"Evil does not need to be promoted. It only needs less self-control to emerge." ~ Roy F. Baumeister

The ability to enact self-restraint and curb our impulses towards violence are moderated by things that push us forward towards harmful behaviour and those that decrease our inherent levels of self-control.

"Such as evil can happen because of an increase in violent impulses or because of a decrease in self-control (or lack of self-control). But in either case, the self-control was not enough to stem the aggressive drives." ~ Roy F. Baumeister.

These influences are summarised in the following diagram[49].

Figure 7 - Factors increasing impulses and preventing restraint

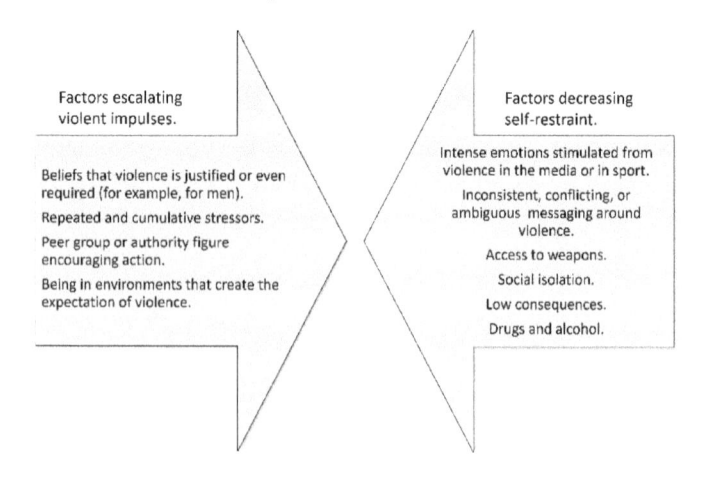

Factors escalating violent impulses.

Beliefs that violence is justified or even required (for example, for men).
Repeated and cumulative stressors.
Peer group or authority figure encouraging action.
Being in environments that create the expectation of violence.

Factors decreasing self-restraint.

Intense emotions stimulated from violence in the media or in sport.
Inconsistent, conflicting, or ambiguous messaging around violence.
Access to weapons.
Social isolation.
Low consequences.
Drugs and alcohol.

Social isolation can significantly reduce an individual's level of self-restraint when it comes to engaging in violent behaviour because it also reduces social accountability and enables a lack of external checks and balances. When individuals are isolated from social networks and supportive relationships, they may feel less bound by social norms and less concerned about the consequences of their actions, which can lead to an increased likelihood of acting on violent impulses. Additionally, isolation can exacerbate feelings of loneliness, frustration, and anger, which can fuel aggressive behaviour and decrease self-control[50].

Alcohol has been shown to impair self-regulation in almost every sphere that has been studied and is well-established as a contributor towards aggression[51]. While alcohol is neither a necessary nor sufficient cause of violence, it has a powerful effect on reducing self-restraint.

There is a more complex relationship, though, between drug use and violence. Research has shown that some drugs are more strongly associated with escalated violence. For instance, stimulants such as methamphetamines and cocaine are particularly noted for their potential to induce aggression. These substances increase dopamine levels in the brain, which can lead to heightened feelings of paranoia, anger, and impulsivity, making violent outbursts more likely.

Prescription medications, particularly certain types of antidepressants and psychotropic drugs, have also been linked to increased risks of violence in some individuals. Selective serotonin reuptake inhibitors (SSRIs), for example, have been associated with violent outbursts in a subset of users, particularly when these drugs are first introduced or discontinued.

These findings underscore the complex relationship between drug use and violence, highlighting the importance of monitoring and managing the use of substances that can exacerbate aggressive tendencies.

Additionally, consumption of high-caffeine energy drinks has been shown to reduce self-restraint and increase levels of self-reported violence. The research found a significant association between high caffeine intake and increased aggression, including physical fights and other conduct disorder behaviours[52]. The findings suggest that excessive consumption of caffeinated beverages may contribute to behavioural problems in adolescents, highlighting the need for greater awareness and regulation of these products among youth.

Undoubtedly, violent behaviour is contributed to by a complex set of variables that interact in unique ways within each individual. However, it does appear that there are some general actions that can be undertaken to help people better regulate their impulses, including:

- Addressing systemic forms of violence causing frustration.
- Publicising positive role models and authority figures.
- Reducing the violent stimulus in media, including sports.
- Ensuring consistent and clear messaging, action and consequences.
- Minimising harm from drugs, alcohol, and high-caffeine drinks.
- Seeking ways to increase social connection.

Core Concepts

We all have violent thoughts and emotions.

There is a gap between feeling the impulse to inflict harm and undertaking the activity.

Choosing not to act in violent ways requires effective self-control.

Violent impulses can be increased by:
- personal beliefs
- peer group pressure
- cumulative stressors
- a person's environment.

Self-control can be inhibited by:
- violence in the media
- inconsistent policies causing confusion
- access to weapons
- social isolation
- lack of consequences
- the effects of drugs and alcohol.

While violence is an individual behaviour, there are structural and systematic supports that can be put in place to help people enact or expand their levels of self-restraint.

8. The Emotions of Violence

"We spend a lot of time judging ourselves harshly for feelings that we had no role in summoning. The only thing you can control is how you handle it." ~ Dan Harris

As shown in the CBMT, emotions are the direct precursor to violent action. So, it is valuable to understand the emotions that can trigger harmful responses. The vast range of different emotions experienced daily can be seen in the Levels of Consciousness Model developed by Dr David Hawkins[53].

Figure 8 - The Levels of Consciousness by Dr David Hawkins

Levels of Consciousness by Dr David Hawkins

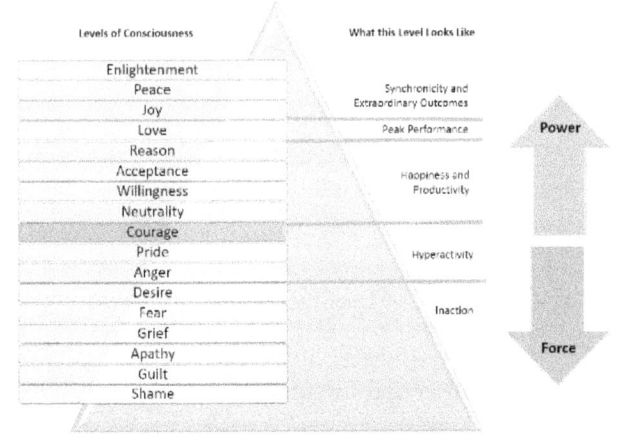

Levels of Consciousness	What this Level Looks Like
Enlightenment	
Peace	Synchronicity and Extraordinary Outcomes
Joy	
Love	Peak Performance
Reason	
Acceptance	Happiness and Productivity
Willingness	
Neutrality	
Courage	
Pride	Hyperactivity
Anger	
Desire	
Fear	Inaction
Grief	
Apathy	
Guilt	
Shame	

Power ↑

Force ↓

Violence is a result of what Dr Hawkins classes as Force Emotions, such as fear, desire and anger. In these emotional states, people feel stressed, overwhelmed and powerless.

These feelings can result in actions to reduce this pressure and reclaim a sense of power. Force emotions are self-centred, divisive, and destructive, creating resistance, conflict, and separation. In contrast, Power Emotions such as willingness, acceptance, reason, and love are life-enhancing and create harmony, unity, and healing. Power Emotions are those that foster happiness and productivity in individual people and across populations.

Two emotions result in hyperactivity and, therefore, can be more likely with people taking overt action to cause harm to others. These are anger and pride.

Anger

"Anger is like a flame blazing up and consuming our self-control, making us think, say, and do things that we will probably regret later." ~ Thich Nhat Hanh

Research consistently links the emotion of anger to aggressive and violent behaviours, both physical and psychological. Anger is an intense emotional state that arises in response to perceived threats, injustices, or frustrations. When anger is not managed effectively, it can escalate into aggression, which is an intention to harm another person. Studies show that anger affects cognitive processes, particularly attention and impulsivity, which can contribute to aggressive behaviour. Individuals with high levels of anger often pay excessive attention to anger-related stimuli and have difficulty disengaging from these stimuli. In this way, anger can be difficult to detect within a person and difficult to de-escalate.

Feeling angry both pushes people towards harmful actions and reduces their own level of self-regulation and inhibition[54]. In terms of behaviour, anger has been linked to both direct physical aggression, such as fighting, and indirect forms of aggression, such as verbal abuse and psychological manipulation.

"Anybody can become angry-that is easy; but to be angry with the right person, and to the right degree, and at the right time, and for the right purpose, and in the right way- that is not within everybody's power and is not easy. "~ Aristotle

Pride

We think of pride as a positive emotion that makes us feel good and compels us to undertake our best efforts. However, while it does have some helpful traits, as Dr Hawkins described, pride is a double-edged sword. It may provide a temporary boost in stimulating, reassuring and empowering self-esteem. Nevertheless, it is also deeply rooted in the ego and can lead to behaviours that are divisive, defensive, aggressive, and ultimately destructive. With pride, people may believe they are better than those around them, possibly resulting in inflated self-esteem.

"People, from playground bullies to warmongering dictators, consist mainly of those who have highly favourable views about themselves. They strike out at others who question or dispute those favourable views." ~ Roy F. Baumeister

Pride-filled individuals who have a strong social dominance orientation can experience ruthless forms of personal unrest such as narcissism and sociopathy, which can predispose them to shamelessly ignore, or even treat with contempt and derision, normal social standards, and to act in their raw self-interest with indifference to the wellbeing of others[55]. As such, and as discussed in Chapter 6, narcissism is an important risk factor for aggression and violence.

Pride often manifests in psychological forms of violence, such as arrogance, condescension, and manipulation. Individuals driven by the protection of pride may belittle others to maintain their sense of superiority. It can lead to toxic dynamics in relationships, where the prideful individual seeks to control or dominate others to preserve their ego.

Pride can also lead to physical violence, particularly in situations where an individual's ego is challenged. For example, in many cultures, defending one's honour or reputation (which is tied to pride) can justify physical aggression. Fights, duels, or retaliatory violence are often driven by the need to "save face" or avoid humiliation. The intense need to protect one's pride can override rational decision-making, leading to impulsive and destructive actions.

There Is No Bad Emotion

Anger and pride may be the precursor to some harmful acts, but they do not always cause violence. The energy from these states can spur helpful actions, too. It can rally people together to protest against systematic injustices, fuel people to seek better and equal treatment and assist them in battling other people's discriminatory and destructive behaviour. Anger and pride have a place, and an important one, in driving us forward to make a better world. The Levels of Consciousness model shows that these emotions are only a few steps away from courage, where fear and force are turned into positive power. Only when these two emotional states are used to justify harm to others does it become an issue.

When subsumed by anger or captured in pride, the powerless can feel compelled to gain power through physical or psychological force. What they see and hear around them can tip them over the line to destruction or help them hold back and find positive ways to address their anger and pride. While emotions are individual, societal support can help people recognise the potential harmful pathways for these emotions and provide accessible and acceptable alternatives to destructive action.

"Let us not look back in anger, nor forward in fear, but around in awareness." ~ James Thurber

Core Concepts

The emotions we feel can be categorised as:
- Force emotions – that are destructive and divisive. They make people feel helpless and powerless.

- Power emotions – are productive and connecting. They enable people to make positive choices and care for themselves and others.

There are two key Force Emotions that drive violent behaviours. These are:
- Anger
- Pride.

Anger pushes people to pay greater attention to anger-related stimuli, making it more difficult to disengage from them.

Pride can lead to people thinking they are separate and better than those around them, and possibly an inflated sense of self-esteem.

Pride-filled individuals can become narcissistic, which is a risk factor for aggression and violence.

Anger and pride can spur positive action when provided with the right support.

9. The Pivotal Role of Shame and Guilt

Shame and guilt are known as the sister emotions. They are similar in that they take up the lowest sections of the Level of Consciousness, suggesting they have the potential to impact a person most negatively. However, they are also at the lowest level of action. For people who have caused harm, these emotions also provide the opportunity to withdraw, reflect and bring about change to prevent violence in the future. They can be seen as an appropriate response to violent behaviour and the start of a shift away from harmful actions.

So, similar to the emotions of anger and pride discussed in the previous chapter, it is not the feelings that are the problem; it is how we respond to them that matters. As we shall see, because shame and guilt relate to the most basic human needs, they must be managed well to ensure they become a source of positive change and not promote further harm.

Shame

Brené Brown defines shame as:

"The intensely painful feeling or experience of believing that we are flawed and therefore unworthy of love and belonging—something we've experienced, done, or failed to do makes us unworthy of connection."

Shame makes individuals think:

"I am a bad person."

When people are subsumed by shame, they feel inherently inferior and incompetent[56]. It makes people fearful of what others will think of them and the impacts on their social standing. It is certainly the way we feel when someone says,

---

"You should be ashamed of yourself."

The Role of Shame in Maintaining Social Norms

Figure 8 shows that Dr David Hawkins places shame at the lowest level on his Map of Consciousness, describing it as the emotional state closest to death. This comparison is understandable, considering our social nature. When you think about our time in tribes, if we were to be ostracised, it would surely lead to death, either at the hands of starvation, dehydration or from being ripped apart by predators. People did not want to be pushed out of the safety of the tribe, and so shame was an internal trigger that made people painfully aware of their failures to meet social or personal standards, thus promoting conformity to group norms. We all have an innate desire to be perceived as attractive and valuable in social settings, so in this way, shame serves an important social function as a regulatory system that discourages violations of moral or social and maintains social order[57].

Shame Counters Pride

Interestingly, shame can work to counter pride, especially hubris, and so counterbalance the inflated self-esteem that is a leading cause of violence. While pride is associated with positive self-assessment, shame is linked to negative self-assessment by exposing vulnerabilities and failures[58]. Therefore, because our brains are predictive, a person will know that hubristic pride could result in a downfall if their shaky foundations of self-esteem are destroyed. The threat of shame then works to discourage behaviours that might lead to social rejection or failure, thus preventing the potentially destructive effects of hubristic pride[59].

The Adverse Responses to Shame

Shame works to strike fear into our most fundamental human need, that of connection with others. Therefore, because it hits at the very core of our being, its deep influence, it can either perpetuate or break the cycle of violence, depending on how it is managed within both individuals and broader social systems. It is well-known that shame can elicit several unhelpful responses when not treated with care. Four in particular have been found in research. These are[60]:

1. Withdrawal - often accompanied by depression, isolation and inaction.
2. Avoidance - a self-centred protectiveness involving an unwillingness to address the issue.
3. Attacking the self - manifesting as psychological or physical self-injury.
4. Attacking others - where the individual lashes out in rage, driven by the need to protect their threatened self-esteem.

None of these responses are helpful in encouraging accountability for one's actions, or responsibility for taking reparative action.

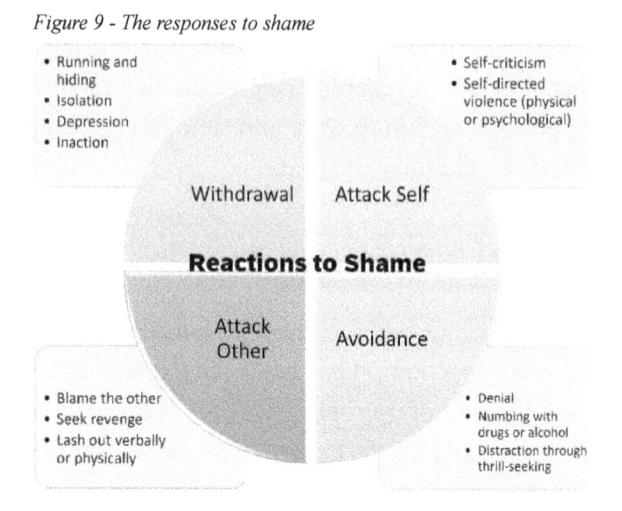

Figure 9 - The responses to shame

Withdrawal
- Running and hiding
- Isolation
- Depression
- Inaction

Attack Self
- Self-criticism
- Self-directed violence (physical or psychological)

Attack Other
- Blame the other
- Seek revenge
- Lash out verbally or physically

Avoidance
- Denial
- Numbing with drugs or alcohol
- Distraction through thrill-seeking

Reactions to Shame

The Shame-Violence Cycle

There is the potential for shame to trigger an attack response, which then creates a destructive shame and violence cycle[61]. The violence causes shame, which causes more violence, and so on. The trigger that shame creates for the person makes them feel like a child in danger, who is about to lose its source of protection, is in peril and so must, through rage, prove its power[62].

"I think the fear of disconnection can make us dangerous." ~ Brené Brown

The fear of disconnection, either from our unrealistic sense of identity or from important relationships, can make shame such a destructive response. It has been found that the "attack other" response to shame is most likely to occur when:

- The individual feels endangered because of the depths to which his self-esteem and sense of competence have been reduced.
- A critical interpersonal relationship has been significantly impaired.

Past experience also comes into play as another contributing factor to adopting the "attack other" response. For example, a person may come from a family system where such behaviour was permitted or even encouraged in dealing with danger.

The way that shame can lead to further violence is shown on the diagram below.

Figure 10 - The shame-violence cycle

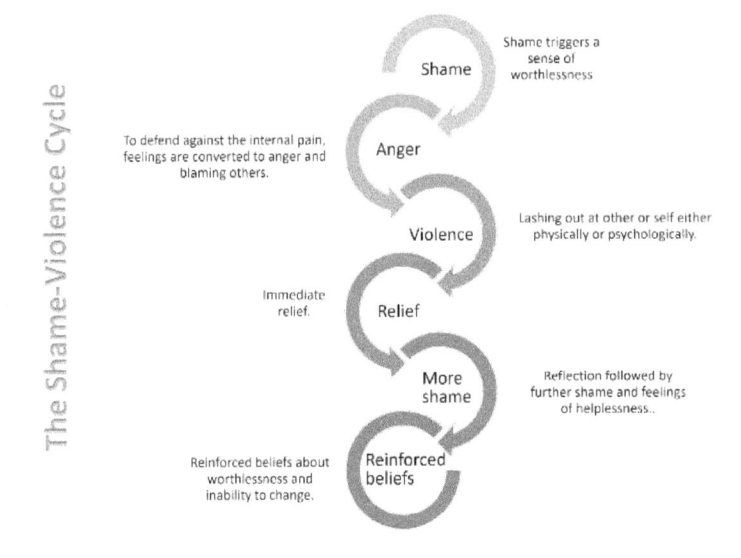

The Shame-Violence Cycle

- **Shame** — Shame triggers a sense of worthlessness
- **Anger** — To defend against the internal pain, feelings are converted to anger and blaming others.
- **Violence** — Lashing out at other or self either physically or psychologically.
- **Relief** — Immediate relief.
- **More shame** — Reflection followed by further shame and feelings of helplessness.
- **Reinforced beliefs** — Reinforced beliefs about worthlessness and inability to change.

The Need for Shame Support

For generations, we have been taught that shame is an appropriate response to being violent and that if we do not feel shameful, then we are broken in some way. So, shame is expected to be a common way in which people respond to the realisation that their actions have been harmful. However, because shame triggers such extreme and primal fears—like the fear of social ostracization—it requires careful management. Without support, those feeling shame are at risk of allowing it to fuel further destructive behaviour towards themselves or others. Thus, it is crucial to provide help and guidance to ensure that shame does not become a catalyst for more violence but rather a stepping stone towards healing and social reintegration.

Guilt

Guilt is the emotion that arises when a person believes they have done something wrong or failed to do something they should have.

"Guilt is an unpleasant feeling with an accompanying belief that one should have felt, thought or acted differently".

Guilt differs from shame in that it focuses on the behaviour rather than the person. In shame, there is the belief that the person who perpetrated the violence is inherently bad. In guilt, it is the behaviour that becomes the issue. For example, someone experiencing guilt would think,

"I did a bad thing."[63]

This distinction is crucial because guilt focuses on the behaviour, offering a path for reparative action. In contrast, shame can feel overwhelming, leaving no clear entry point for change and potentially justifying continued negative behaviour[64]. If people consider themselves bad, they are more likely to use this as an excuse to continue doing bad things – after all, it is just who they are.

The Role of Guilt in Maintaining Social Norms

Guilt is uncomfortable, yet it plays a vital role in maintaining social stability by encouraging individuals to adhere to communal values.

> *"Guilt is a strongly prosocial behaviour that underpins our communities."* ~ Roy F. Baumeister

Guilt is important in promoting cooperative behaviour and social harmony as it helps people recognise when they have done something wrong and often motivates individuals to make amends, thus reinforcing social norms and relationships. Unlike shame, which would cast people out of the community, guilt brings them in, identifies the action that has caused harm, and asks them to make amends.

The Potential Positive Outcomes of Guilt

Guilt is typically linked to specific actions or omissions, making it easier for individuals to identify reparative actions. Unlike shame, which can be paralysing due to its focus on the self, guilt allows a person to focus on correcting the behaviour that led to the guilt. This focus on behaviour rather than self-worth provides a clear path to reconciliation, whether through apologies, compensation, or other forms of making amends[65]. In this way, guilt encourages self-reflection, taking personal responsibility, and engaging in reparative actions that can prevent future harm.

"I believe that guilt is adaptive and helpful—it's holding something we've done or failed to do up against our values and feeling psychological discomfort." ~ Brené Brown

Research has shown that the constructive management of guilt is an incredibly effective tool to prevent further violent behaviour[66]. When individuals authentically assume responsibility for their actions and experience moral feelings of guilt, aggressive behaviour can be deterred. When individuals are aware of their guilt and respond to it constructively—such as acknowledging wrongdoing and seeking to make amends—it can lead to positive outcomes and reduce the likelihood of recurring violence.

When Guilt Becomes Maladaptive

Guilt, however, can also become unhelpful, particularly when it is intense or unresolved. In such cases, guilt can lead to long-lasting self-destructive behaviours or externalised violence. When this occurs, it is called "maladaptive guilt". This type of guilt, often associated with trauma or perceived moral failings, can drive individuals to aggressive actions either as a form of self-punishment or as a way to cope with the intense emotional burden.

For instance, if reparative actions are not available, the emotional burden of guilt can become so heavy that it slips the person into shame. A person may also rise to anger at themselves for their actions and undertake acts of self-harm, such as substance abuse, which too may lead to more aggressive behaviour.

Where guilt is linked with perceptions of injustice, there can also be a desire for revenge, which often manifests in aggressive behaviour. This desire is especially pertinent in contexts where individuals feel wronged or blame themselves for negative outcomes, driving them to take violent actions as a way to restore their sense of justice or self-worth. So, while guilt has the potential to be an uncomfortable and yet productive emotion, if not supported positively, it can also perpetuate violence on self or others.

Managing Guilt

The impact of guilt on behaviour—whether it leads to positive change or exacerbates negative behaviour—depends largely on how it is managed. When guilt is focused on behaviour and individuals are supported in identifying and engaging in reparative actions, it can be a powerful force for good. However, when guilt becomes overwhelming or is not accompanied by clear avenues for making amends, it can become maladaptive, leading to further destructive behaviour.

The degree to which individuals are aware of and authentically respond to their feelings of guilt can significantly influence whether these feelings will lead to nonviolent resolutions. Programs that emphasise the recognition of guilt and promote its constructive management are more likely to succeed in preventing further violence.

The Misuse of Shame and Guilt

Shame can be helpful in breaking the cycle of violence by showing people that what they have done is not socially acceptable. However, because of its blanket approach to the person can lead to depression and helplessness or reactionary violence. Either way, both the person experiencing the shame and the people around them suffer. Guilt is a more positive response as reparative actions can be found that put the perpetrator in a more positive and responsible frame of mind. They can take action to repair their wrongdoing and learn to take more personal responsibility in the future. However, it can also become maladaptive when the emotional burden is long-lasting or overwhelming.

Because of the intense effects of shame and guilt, these emotions cannot only become treatments for violent action but also sources of psychological torture. Shame and guilt can be used as tools of psychological violence that perpetrators can use to inflict harm. Those in power can apply it to reinforce theirs and prevent other people's potential, suppress others and gain advantage in some way.

In Abusive Relationships

For example, in abusive relationships, shame and guilt are often wielded as tools of psychological torture by one partner to control and manipulate the other. For instance, an abusive partner might constantly berate their victim, instilling a sense of shame by convincing them that they are inherently flawed, worthless, or responsible for the abuser's unhappiness. This emotional abuse creates a cycle of dependency where the victim feels trapped, believing they deserve the mistreatment due to their perceived failures. The abuser may also use guilt to keep the victim submissive, for example, by blaming them for any conflicts in the relationship or for "making" the abuser act violently. The victim's guilt and shame reinforce their sense of powerlessness and make it more difficult for them to leave the abusive relationship, effectively trapping them in a cycle of psychological torture.

Against Indigenous People

Colonisers historically imposed a profound sense of shame on Indigenous cultures, a practice that has had long-lasting effects that continue to resonate today. During colonisation, Indigenous peoples were often made to feel ashamed of their cultural practices, languages, and identities. Colonizers frequently portrayed Indigenous ways of life as "primitive" or "inferior" to European norms, leading to the systematic devaluation of Indigenous cultures and the internalisation of a sense of shame. This cultural shaming was reinforced through policies like the forced removal of Indigenous children from their families to attend residential schools, where they were punished for speaking their native languages or practising their traditions.

The legacy of this imposed shame is still felt today. Many Indigenous people struggle with internalised shame about their cultural identity, a direct result of generations of enforced assimilation and denigration. This shame has contributed to high rates of mental health issues, substance abuse, and social dislocation within Indigenous communities. The shame imposed by colonisers also manifests in the ongoing marginalisation of Indigenous cultures in mainstream society, where Indigenous languages and traditions are often still undervalued or ignored.

Efforts to revitalise Indigenous cultures and languages are ongoing, but the scars of imposed shame are deep. These efforts include cultural revival programs, land rights movements, and truth and reconciliation commissions that aim to address the historical wrongs and heal the collective trauma experienced by Indigenous peoples.

This imposed shame serves as a reminder of the powerful and lasting impact of psychological violence at the societal level, where entire cultures have been made to feel inferior and disconnected from their heritage. The work to overcome this legacy continues as Indigenous peoples reclaim and celebrate their identities despite the historical efforts to suppress them.

"As Aboriginal people we have always retained our resilience, our humour and our cultural integrity – we will always retain our dreams and a vision for the future for our people." ~ Ken Wyatt

Core Concepts

Shame and guilt are known as prosocial behaviours – they create signals to show us we have done something outside the boundaries of society and our own moral code.

Shame is the belief that "I am a bad person." It is a risky response to violence as it can cause more frustration and aggression, leading to a violence/shame cycle.

Shame can be a motivator for reflection and change, but it does need to be managed well.

Guilt is the belief that "I have done something bad". Because it is linked to behaviour, it is more likely to lead to remorse and reparative actions.

However, guilt too can become maladaptive when it is intense or unresolved, and this can push people to punish themselves or others.

Shame and guilt are not only antidotes to violence. People can use them as a form of psychological violence against others, for example in:

- Abusive relationships – where the perpetrator uses shame and guilt to make the other person feel flawed and responsible for their harmful behaviour.

- Colonisation – where colonial policies made Indigenous people feel their cultures were inferior, with generations still struggling with internalised shame.

10. Breaking the Cycle of Violence

Because violence is a behaviour, it can be changed. It is possible to break the cycle of violence and stop it from spiralling downwards. As shown in the Dr Hawkins Model, there is a bridge that helps people rise from the destructive and negative states of being (the Force emotions) to more empowering ones, where people find their own positive power. This transition state is courage.

The Role of Courage

If you look the word courage up in the dictionary, you will see that the definition of courage is:

"The ability to do something that frightens one." [67]

This definition holds the key to what courage is all about. Courage does not mean that you don't feel afraid. In fact, it is the exact opposite. Fear is inherent; in fact, bravery does not exist without fear. But courage is making a choice to move beyond fear. It is the choice to sit in the discomfort of the unknown because there is something more important.

As we have previously seen, fear plays an integral role in violence, as so many perpetrators feel threatened in some way before they choose to harm themselves or others. Courage is essential to move beyond reactive or habitual actions into those that are helpful to the person and all those around them. It is vital to help people become aware that there is an alternative and to help them take responsibility for their actions and make changes.

"Courage is not the absence of fear, but rather the assessment that something else is more important than fear."
~ Franklin D. Roosevelt

As this definition suggests, courage is not a quality endowed at birth or something our Fairy Godmother grants us with a wave of a wand. It is an ability that is developed over time and with dedicated practice. Like reading, driving a car or playing an instrument, finding courage and breaking the cycle of violence is a skill you learn over time.

There are three key steps in gaining the courage to change.

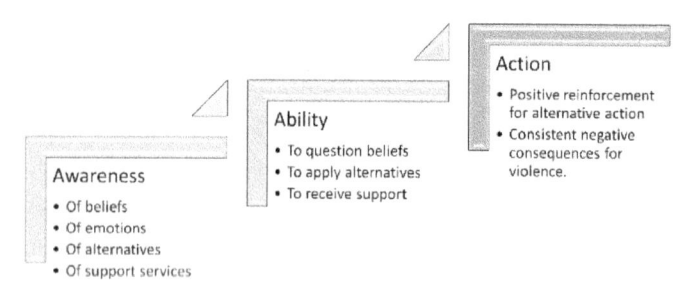

Figure 11 - The three steps to break the cycle

Awareness
- Of beliefs
- Of emotions
- Of alternatives
- Of support services

Ability
- To question beliefs
- To apply alternatives
- To receive support

Action
- Positive reinforcement for alternative action
- Consistent negative consequences for violence.

Awareness

For a person to make change, they first need to be aware that their beliefs or behaviours are problematic. Unfortunately, with violence, this may only occur after significant damage has been done and they are pushed to reflect and question their assumptions and actions. It isn't easy to achieve the first step of awareness when there are:

- Cultural cues legitimising violence in many forms.
- Peer groups who push violence as a valid way of solving problems
- Positive reinforcements (or a lack of negative consequences) for people who perpetrate physical or psychological violence.

One key thing that prevents awareness of harmful beliefs and behaviours is desensitisation[68]. The more people get used to violence, the more it becomes embedded in our society in all its various forms and the more it becomes the new norm. Therefore, consistent education and messaging about what violence is and the constant criticism of it in all its forms vital. When there is confusion, awareness and judgment become clouded, making it more difficult to make an alternate choice.

Awareness of one's emotional state is also important so that interventions can be applied before they become too intense and overwhelming, resulting in destructive action. However, awareness is almost impossible when a person is under the influence of alcohol or drugs, is being excited by sports or other electronic media, or is being pushed on by peer groups.

Finally, for people to make a change, they need to be aware that there are alternative means to achieving their aims and solving their problems. This may seem obvious to a person in a peaceful, supportive place. However, when someone truly feels they are under threat, their fight-or-flight response can be in overdrive, and it can be difficult to deescalate and search for substitutes for violence. In the awareness stage, we aim to arm people with a ready set of alternatives, increasing their alternative capacity.

Ability

It is one thing to be aware of beliefs, emotions, and alternative behaviours, but another great leap to have the ability to do things differently. Similar to awareness, ability is supported at individual and societal levels. It takes individual introspection as well as critical cultural conversations to enable someone to question what they think about violence and how they may already perpetrate it in their own lives.

It takes supportive family, friends, workplaces and health services to enable people to practice alternatives to all forms of psychological and physical violence and to apply them in their everyday lives. Only practice makes perfect, and supportive frameworks need to be in place to provide feedback and reflection to facilitate change.

Moreover, people need to be able to gain support when and where they need it. Support is not just needed for the physical forms of violence that gain great attention but for those people who may be resorting to psychological violence to solve a problem. They, too, need to be able to speak to someone to assist them to deescalate and move away from their harmful behaviour.

Action

For changes to stick, constant reinforcement is necessary. Reinforcement can take the form of supportive people and institutions who continually provide space and supervisors to facilitate the practice of positive behaviours. At both an individual and a societal level, acknowledgement and celebration of alternative approaches to problem-solving and goal attainment is critical. As is consistent and dedicated discouragement of and penalties for physical and psychological violence.

Violent action becomes more likely to be repeated when bystanders, the police or the community fails to intervene or the victim fails to react [69].

In both of these situations, the perpetrator feels like they have "gotten away with it," which is likely to reinforce their belief that the violence was justified. The lack of consequences means they are more likely to choose a similar violent response the next time they encounter an issue. After all, if it worked the first time, why not try it the second?

Breaking the Cycle at Every Stage

Awareness, ability, and action can be applied and strengthened at every stage of the CBTM to bring about positive change. The diagram below provides an overview of how this can be achieved at the individual and societal levels, with further detail provided in the following chapters. However, the further we can make change towards the beginning of the cycle, that is, in beliefs, the more effective and sustainable change will be. Additionally, while ultimately, individuals are responsible for their own behaviour, the culture in which we live and the consequences we experience for harmful actions are a function of a whole range of government policies and social practices.

UNDERSTANDING VIOLENCE

Figure 12 - Breaking the cycle at each stage

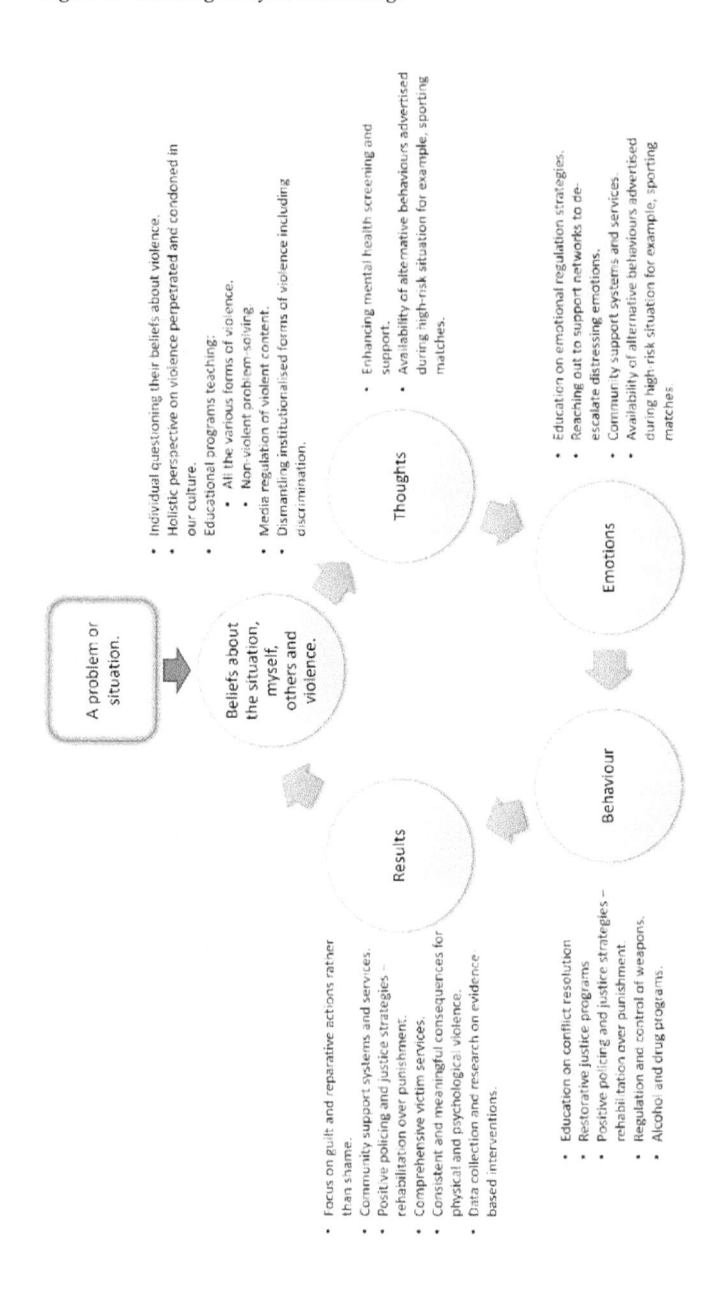

A problem or situation.

Beliefs about the situation, myself, others and violence.

Thoughts
- Individual questioning their beliefs about violence.
- Holistic perspective on violence perpetrated and condoned in our culture.
- Educational programs teaching:
  - All the various forms of violence.
  - Non-violent problem-solving
- Media regulation of violent content.
- Dismantling institutionalised forms of violence including discrimination.

Emotions
- Enhancing mental health screening and support.
- Availability of alternative behaviours advertised during high-risk situation for example, sporting matches.
- Education on emotional regulation strategies.
- Reaching out to support networks to de-escalate distressing emotions.
- Community support systems and services.
- Availability of alternative behaviours advertised during high-risk situation for example, sporting matches.

Behaviour
- Education on conflict resolution
- Restorative justice programs
- Positive policing and justice strategies – rehabilitation over punishment.
- Regulation and control of weapons.
- Alcohol and drug programs.

Results
- Focus on guilt and reparative actions rather than shame.
- Community support systems and services.
- Positive policing and justice strategies – rehabilitation over punishment.
- Comprehensive victim services.
- Consistent and meaningful consequences for physical and psychological violence.
- Data collection and research on evidence based interventions.

Decreasing Impulse and Increasing Restraint

Another way to think about breaking the cycle of violence is to work concurrently on the following:

- Reducing the impulses towards violence.
- Increasing the level of self-restraint to enact violence.

As shown in Chapter 7, there are things that compel people towards violent behaviours, either physical or psychological and things that reduce the ability to respond in less harmful ways. Both levers, push and pull, can be used to make violence a less automatic and immediate response. Here are some ways both sides of the violent equation can be addressed at the individual and societal levels, leading to a holistic preventative program.

Figure 13 - Individual-level interventions

Individual Level Interventions	
Decreasing Violent Impulses	**Increasing Self-Restraint**
Identify beliefs about violence and how these may be driving behaviour	Identify and practice alternatives to violence.
Understand psychological violence and how it plays out and may be perpetrated.	Strengthen problem-solving skills.
Learn techniques for stress management and emotional regulation.	Avoid isolation.
Avoid time with peers that promote violence.	Establish accountability mechanisms for positive behaviours.
Establish social and support networks with positive people.	Reduce exposure to inciting media for example, violent sport, games and shows.
	Avoid substances that reduce self-restraint for example, drugs and alcohol and high-caffeine energy drinks.

Figure 14 - Societal-level interventions

Societal Level Interventions	
Decreasing Violent Impulses	**Increasing Self-Restraint**
Awareness campaigns highlighting and countering harmful beliefs about violence.	Promotion of positive role-models who demonstrate non-violent problem-solving.
Increase recognition for psychological violence and its harms.	Strengthen family support programs that teach parents how to model and reinforce self-control in their children.
Education on positive conflict resolution skills (starting in early childhood).	Rehabilitation programs for offenders that focus on self-control and decision-making.
Consistent naming and consequences for violence in the public domain (for example, in politics).	Regulation to reduce exposure to and normalisation of violence in the media for example, violent sport, games and shows.
Ready access to support services for stress management and emotional regulation.	Expand programs aimed at reducing alcohol and drug abuse and access to high-caffeine energy drinks.
Community programs that support positive outlets for stress and building peer support.	
Addressing systematic forms of violence that are causing frustration for example, discrimination, racism, inequality.	

Core Concepts

Breaking the cycle of violence requires courage:
- At an individual level, to challenge beliefs and behaviours.
- At a societal level, to identify how much violence is embedded into our culture.

Courage moves people away from fear-based and aggressive states towards helpful actions.

Building courage requires:
- Awareness
- Ability
- Action.

Desentisation reduces the level of awareness of violence. Violence becomes the norm, and people stop seeing it. Desentisation makes tackling violence more difficult.

Changing beliefs and behaviours takes repetition, so support needs to be in place to help people practice more positive ways to solve problems and achieve their aims.

Consistent, clear and meaningful consequences need to be in place for all forms of physical and psychological violence.

The cycle of behaviour can be broken at any stage; however, intervening at beliefs increases the effectiveness and sustainability of change.

Breaking the cycle of behaviour requires concurrent and synchronistic interventions to both:
- Reduce violent impulses.
- Increase self-restraint.

11. The Futility of Fear-Based Approaches

"Hate begets hate; violence begets violence; toughness begets a greater toughness. We must meet the forces of hate with the power of love." ~ Martin Luther King Jr.

Fear-based approaches have been at the forefront of government and community efforts to reduce violence for centuries. It makes sense that instilling fear will deter individuals from undertaking activities outside the societal code of conduct. Following this assumption, there is a simple extrapolation: the more severe the consequences, the more effective the deterrent. This belief is the foundation upon which our policing and justice systems have been built. It has resulted in the implementation of the following forms of fear-based approaches to violence:
- Punitive justice systems.
- Scare tactics in education.
- Aggressive policing.

Punitive Justice Systems

One of the most prominent examples of fear-based strategies is found in punitive justice systems, particularly those that emphasise harsh sentencing and "tough on crime" policies. These systems rely on the notion that severe penalties, such as mandatory minimum sentences, three-strikes laws, strict parole and detention practices, will deter individuals from committing crimes out of fear of the consequences.

Mandatory Minimum Sentencing

Australia has enacted mandatory minimum sentencing laws, particularly in relation to drug offences, firearm possession, and certain violent crimes. These laws require judges to impose a minimum sentence regardless of the individual circumstances of the case. Critics argue that mandatory minimum sentences remove judicial discretion, often leading to disproportionately harsh punishments that do not fit the crime. These laws have been particularly controversial in cases involving Indigenous Australians, who are disproportionately affected by such policies. Research also indicates that harsher prison conditions and longer sentences do not effectively reduce recidivism, highlighting the limitations of punitive justice as a fear-based deterrent[70].

"Three Strikes" Laws

Australia has implemented "three strikes" laws in some jurisdictions, where individuals convicted of a third serious offence receive a significantly harsher sentence, often life imprisonment. These laws have been criticised for contributing to prison overcrowding and failing to address the root causes of criminal behaviour.

Strict Bail and Parole Laws

Australia has increasingly adopted stricter bail and parole laws, which make it more difficult for accused individuals to be released before their trial or for convicted individuals to be granted early release. These laws are often justified by the need to protect public safety. The tightening of bail laws in Victoria following the 2017 Bourke Street attack, where the accused was out on bail, is an example of how fear-driven responses to high-profile incidents can lead to more punitive policies.

However, stricter bail and parole laws can lead to prolonged periods of pre-trial detention, even for individuals who are ultimately acquitted or convicted of minor offences. This approach has been criticised for contributing to overcrowded prisons and exacerbating the issues faced by vulnerable populations, such as mental health and substance abuse problems.

Youth Detention Practices

In some Australian states, there have been reports of harsh treatment of juveniles in detention, with punitive measures being employed as a form of discipline, including isolation and physical restraints. Human rights organisations have widely condemned such punitive practices in youth detention centres for their potential to cause long-term psychological harm and for failing to rehabilitate young offenders. These practices can perpetuate a cycle of violence and criminal behaviour rather than addressing its root causes.

Scare Tactics in Education

Fear-based approaches are also prevalent in educational settings, particularly in programs designed to deter youth from engaging in criminal behaviour. One example is taking at-risk youth on tours of prisons or detention centres and exposing them to the harsh realities of life behind bars. The idea is that by instilling fear of incarceration, these programs will deter young people from committing crimes.

However, research on the effectiveness of such programs has been overwhelmingly negative. Studies have consistently found that these programs do not reduce criminal behaviour and may increase the likelihood of future criminal activity. A meta-analysis found that participants in programs that engaged in such scare tactics were more likely to engage in criminal behaviour than those who did not participate, suggesting that scare tactics can backfire by reinforcing criminal identities rather than deterring them[71].

Zero-tolerance policies in schools represent another fear-based strategy. These policies mandate harsh penalties, such as suspension or expulsion, for various infractions, including minor offences. While intended to maintain order and safety, zero-tolerance policies have been criticised for disproportionately affecting minority students and contributing to the "school-to-prison pipeline." Research indicates that these policies can lead to negative outcomes, including higher dropout rates and increased involvement in the juvenile justice system[72].

"Nothing good ever comes from fear." ~ Nelson Mandela

Aggressive Policing Tactics

Similar to the assumptions around harsh penalties, aggressive policing tactics are based on the belief that the use of excessive force will maintain order. For example, the visible display of weapons by police can create a sense of intimidation, leading to compliance in some instances. However, it can also provoke fear and aggression, particularly in high-stress situations, potentially leading to an escalation of violence rather than its reduction[73].

Historically, aggressive tactics have been used to manage large-scale pickets and protests, particularly in the context of industrial actions. In some cases, police intervention escalated conflicts, resulting in violent clashes. During the COVID-19 lockdowns, police used aggressive tactics against anti-lockdown protesters. These included the deployment of riot police and heavy-handed measures, leading to widespread criticism regarding the disproportionate use of force and the use of policing to override civil liberties.

Fear-Based Approaches Don't Work

One must ask what the ultimate goal of our justice and educational system is. Is it to reduce violence? If so, then fear-based approaches are missing the mark.

There is mounting evidence challenging the effectiveness of fear as a tool for promoting lasting behavioural change because:

They exacerbate the sense of threat that underlies violent behaviour. As we have heard, most perpetrators of violence are in a state of fear, and violence is used as a way to reduce their feelings of threat. By exacerbating their sense of fear, punitive measures, scare tactics, and aggressive policing can increase the likelihood of ongoing violent behaviour. The cycle of fear and violence is why, in many cases, fear-based approaches can exacerbate the very problems they aim to solve, leading to increased aggression, resistance, and recidivism[74].

They deal with behaviours, not beliefs. While fear-based tactics may produce immediate behavioural compliance, they fail to address the underlying beliefs and conditions that lead to violence in the first place. As we have seen in Chapter 6, the cycle of violence is fuelled by a complex set of beliefs about oneself, the situation and violence. Without addressing the foundations upon which violence stands, then any behavioural change will not be sustainable.

A key piece of evidence for the fact that fear-based approaches don't work comes from the United States, where, in some states, people are faced with the threat of losing their lives for criminal activities. Death is the harshest of penalties, so one would think that if extreme punishments were the answer, these jurisdictions would be free of crime. However, research suggests that the death penalty may have little to no impact on crime rates, challenging the assumption that fear of execution deters criminal behaviour[75].

Balancing Accountability and Support

Effectively addressing violent behaviour requires a balance between accountability and support. Rather than relying solely on punitive measures, which often fail to produce lasting change, there is a growing recognition of the importance of restorative justice and personal responsibility in fostering genuine behavioural transformation.

Restorative Justice
Restorative justice is an approach that emphasises accountability while fostering understanding, healing, and reconciliation. Unlike traditional punitive systems, which focus on retribution, restorative justice seeks to repair the

harm caused by violence by involving all stakeholders—victims, offenders, and the community—in the process of justice. This approach allows offenders to take responsibility for their actions, understand the impact of their behaviour on others, and actively participate in making amends.

Research has shown that restorative justice programs can lead to lower recidivism rates and higher satisfaction among victims compared to traditional justice systems. A meta-analysis has found that restorative justice programs are associated with a significant reduction in reoffending, particularly when offenders are genuinely engaged in the process[76]. These programs emphasise the humanisation of justice, where offenders are treated not just as criminals but as individuals capable of change.

Personal Responsibility

Encouraging individuals to take personal responsibility for their actions within a supportive framework is crucial in addressing violent behaviour. When people are held accountable in a way that promotes understanding and empathy, they are more likely to recognise the harm they have caused and take steps to change their behaviour. This approach moves away from fear-based compliance and towards fostering intrinsic motivation for change.

Supportive interventions, such as cognitive-behavioural therapy (CBT) and mentorship programs, help individuals understand the root causes of their violent behaviour, whether they stem from past trauma, social conditioning, or other factors. By providing tools and support for personal growth, these interventions empower individuals to take responsibility for their actions and make positive changes in their lives.

Effective Consequences

Consequences for violent behaviour should be meaningful and focused on rehabilitation rather than mere punishment. Effective consequences involve addressing the underlying issues that lead to violence, such as unresolved anger, lack of coping skills, or distorted beliefs about power and control. Rehabilitation-focused consequences can include mandatory counselling, community service, or participation in restorative justice circles.

Research supports the effectiveness of rehabilitation-focused approaches over punitive measures. Studies have shown that when consequences are designed to promote learning and personal development, they are more likely to lead to lasting behaviour change. For example, programs that combine accountability with skill-building and emotional support have been found to reduce reoffending and improve social outcomes for offenders[77].

The Power of Love

If Martin Luther King Jr. was correct, we should develop policies and programs founded on love instead of taking fear-based approaches to violence. Love can be seen as an airy-fairy concept and spur associations with leniency. However, the definition of love is:

"The action taken to reduce suffering, bring happiness, and enable the self or other to achieve their fullest potential." ~ Belinda Tobin

There is nothing "soft" about this definition. It requires committed action to help people overcome their challenges, reduce the sources of suffering that are causing the violent behaviour and enable them to be their very best. There is a saying that:

"Hurt people hurt people."

Therefore, if we want to get to the root of violence, we need to help them overcome the things keeping them stuck in a sense of shame, fear and anger and help them move to a place of courage to question their beliefs and take responsibility for their behaviour.

Core Concepts

Fear-based approaches to violence include:
- Punitive justice systems – minimum sentencing, strict bail and parole laws, three strikes and youth detention.
- Scare tactics in education – including introducing at-risk offenders to the realities of life in prison or detention and zero-tolerance policies.
- Aggressive police tactics – brandishing weapons and excessive use of force.

Such programs and practices may lead to short-term compliance but do not result in reduced violence.

They are ineffective because they:
- Exacerbate the sense of threat that sits behind violent behaviour.
- Do not address the underlying beliefs around violence.

Effectively addressing violent behaviour requires a balance between accountability and support.

Effective responses include:
- Restorative justice
- Taking personal responsibility
- Consequences focused on rehabilitation over punishment.

Love is:
"The action taken to reduce suffering, bring happiness, and enable the self or other to achieve their fullest potential." It is not a soft concept but a requirement to reduce violence.

Hurt people hurt people. Therefore, if we want to get to the root of violence, we need to help them:
- Overcome the things keeping them stuck in a sense of shame, fear and anger.
- Move to a place of courage to question their beliefs and take responsibility for their behaviour.

12. Violence from a Public Health Perspective

> *"I've always been interested in public health approaches because it seems to me we have this yearning for silver bullets, and that is not in fact how change comes about. Change comes through silver buckshot — a lot of little things that achieve results. That's a classic public health approach."* ~ Nicholas Kristof

Violence is traditionally viewed through the lenses of criminal justice and law enforcement. However, neither of these perspectives have been successful in reducing its quantum or severity. Instead, violence is increasingly recognised as a public health issue. This shift in perspective reflects the understanding that violence, like a disease, spreads through populations, affects individuals and communities, and requires preventive rather than merely reactive strategies. When violence is seen as a public health issue, it opens up new avenues for intervention that focus on prevention, education, and community involvement rather than solely on punishment.

The impact of violence extends far beyond the immediate physical harm to victims; it affects mental health, disrupts community cohesion, and strains healthcare systems. Communities afflicted by high levels of violence experience increased healthcare costs, reduced quality of life, and long-term social and economic repercussions. Recognising this, various regions and organisations have begun to address violence using public health models, which emphasise prevention, early intervention, and the systemic factors contributing to violence.

The Public Health Model for Violence Prevention

The public health model approaches violence prevention by addressing the root causes and broader social determinants of violence. This model operates on three levels:

Primary Prevention: Involves strategies to prevent violence before it occurs by addressing risk factors and strengthening protective factors within communities. These include educational programs, community engagement initiatives, and policies aimed at reducing inequality and social isolation.

Secondary Prevention: Focuses on immediate responses to violence, including interventions that reduce the impact of violence after it occurs. Examples include emergency healthcare services, crisis intervention, and rapid response teams designed to de-escalate potentially violent situations.

Tertiary Prevention: Aims to reduce the long-term effects of violence by providing rehabilitation and support services to victims and perpetrators. Tertiary prevention can include counselling, mental health services, and community reintegration programs.

The public health approach also emphasises data collection and analysis, enabling authorities to identify patterns, assess risks, and tailor interventions to specific populations. By understanding who is most at risk and why, public health officials can design targeted prevention strategies that address the unique needs of different communities.

The Impact of the Public Health Perspective

Viewing violence through the lens of public health has several significant benefits. First, it shifts the focus from punitive measures to preventive ones, recognising that preventing violence before it occurs is more effective and less costly than responding to it after the fact. This approach also emphasises the need for early intervention, particularly with at-risk populations, to prevent the development of violent behaviours.

Additionally, treating violence as a public health issue encourages a broader societal response. It calls for the involvement of healthcare providers, educators, community leaders, and policymakers, all of whom play a role in preventing violence. This collaborative approach helps to address the root causes of violence, such as poverty, inequality, and social isolation. It creates a more supportive environment for those at risk.

However, this approach has its challenges. It requires significant resources, including funding for research, education, and community programs. Additionally, it demands a cultural shift in how society views and responds to violence, moving away from punishment and toward prevention and rehabilitation.

The pros and cons of taking a public health approach to violence are outlined in the following table.

Figure 15 – Pros and cons of the public health perspective to violence

Pros and Cons of the Public Health Perspective	
Pros	**Cons**
Prevention Focus: Emphasizes early intervention and prevention, reducing the likelihood of violence occurring in the first place.	**Resource Intensive**: Requires significant investment in public health infrastructure, data collection, and community programs.
Holistic Approach: Addresses the root causes of violence, including social determinants like poverty, inequality, and mental health.	**Cultural Shift Required**: Needs a shift in societal attitudes from punitive to preventive approaches, which can be challenging to achieve.
Collaboration: Encourages cross-sector collaboration, involving healthcare, education, law enforcement, and community organizations.	**Implementation Challenges**: Coordinating efforts across multiple sectors and maintaining consistent, long-term funding and support can be difficult.
Community Engagement: Involves communities in the solution, fostering social cohesion and local ownership of violence prevention efforts.	**Measuring Success**: Prevention outcomes are harder to measure than immediate punitive outcomes, making it challenging to demonstrate effectiveness quickly.
Empowerment and Healing: Shifting from viewing violence less as a personal failing and more like a disease reduces the shame which can fuel further violence.	**Risk of Oversimplification**: May risk oversimplifying violence by focusing too much on health-related factors and not enough on individual accountability and justice.
Cost-Effective: Preventing violence can be more cost-effective than dealing with its consequences, reducing long-term healthcare and criminal justice costs.	

Examples of Defining Violence as a Public Health Issue

Despite the difficulties in implementing a public health perspective on violence, several regions and organisations worldwide have demonstrated the effectiveness of this strategy.

Scotland's Violence Reduction Unit (VRU)[78]

Scotland's Violence Reduction Unit (VRU) is a leading example of addressing violence through a public health lens. Established in 2005 in response to high levels of knife crime and violence, the VRU treats violence as a preventable disease. Scotland has seen a dramatic reduction in violent crime by focusing on education, rehabilitation, and community engagement. The VRU's success underscores the importance of treating violence as a public health issue rather than just a criminal justice problem.

World Health Organisation (WHO)[79]

The WHO has recognised violence as a major public health concern globally. The organisation's "World Report on Violence and Health" (2002) was a groundbreaking document that framed violence as a public health issue and provided a comprehensive analysis of the causes, effects, and potential interventions for various forms of violence, including interpersonal, self-directed, and collective violence. The WHO continues to support countries in developing and implementing public health strategies to prevent violence, focusing on education, community programs, and policy reforms.

United States (CDC)[80]

The Centres for Disease Control and Prevention (CDC) in the United States has been at the forefront of treating violence as a public health issue. The CDC's Division of Violence Prevention conducts research, develops guidelines, and provides resources for preventing violence at the community and national levels. The CDC's public health approach emphasises early intervention, particularly in youth, to prevent the development of violent behaviours later in life. Programs like "Striving to Reduce Youth Violence Everywhere" (STRYVE) aim to reduce youth violence through community engagement, education, and policy change.

New Zealand[81]

New Zealand has integrated public health strategies into its family violence prevention programs. The country's holistic approach includes initiatives like the "It's Not OK" campaign, which uses public awareness and community engagement to shift cultural attitudes toward violence. New Zealand's approach also includes specialised family violence courts and community-based support services, all underpinned by a public health perspective emphasising prevention and early intervention.

Core Concepts

Violence is increasingly recognised as a public health issue.

From a public health perspective, violence is treated like a disease that spreads through populations, affects individuals and communities, and requires both preventive and reactive strategies.

As a public health issue, new interventions, including those focusing on prevention, education, and community involvement, become available.

Preventing violence can be more cost-effective than dealing with its consequences, reducing long-term healthcare and criminal justice costs.

Implementing the public health perspective is resource-intensive to bring about cultural change and requires collaboration across agencies.

Despite the difficulties in implementing a public health perspective on violence, there are several regions and organisations around the world have demonstrated the effectiveness of this strategy, including:
- Scotland's Violence Reduction Unit (VRU)
- World Health Organisation (WHO)
- The United States Centre for Disease Control and Prevention (CDC)
- New Zealand family violence prevention programs.

13. How Economic Policy Exacerbates Violence

> *"Today, our society is caught in the grip of superficial values – glamour, glitter, materialism, a pathological emphasis on youth, a neglect of the elderly, the handicapped. Families are being broken up under the impact of a frenzied desire for success." ~ Patrick J Carnes*

Economic policy is not often seen as an obvious contributor to violent cultures. Still, recent research has shown that it does play a part, namely through its influence over the level of materialism within a society. For where materialism increases, so does aggression.

What is Materialism?

Materialism is the belief that wellbeing and happiness are primarily derived from acquiring and possessing material goods[82]. In materialistic cultures, individuals are socialised to believe that tangible possessions are not only symbols of success but also crucial to self-identity and social status. People begin to define themselves by what they own and tend to gain a sense of self-worth through comparison of their possessions against others.

The Negative Consequences of Materialism

Everyone likes to have nice things, but when materialism is present, the need for possessions becomes ingrained in an individual's identity. So, instead of bringing joy and pleasure into people's lives, materialism often leads to lower psychological wellbeing and higher levels of stress and anxiety, potentially fuelling anger, aggression and violence[83]. It does this through the following:

Figure 16 – The negative consequences of materialism

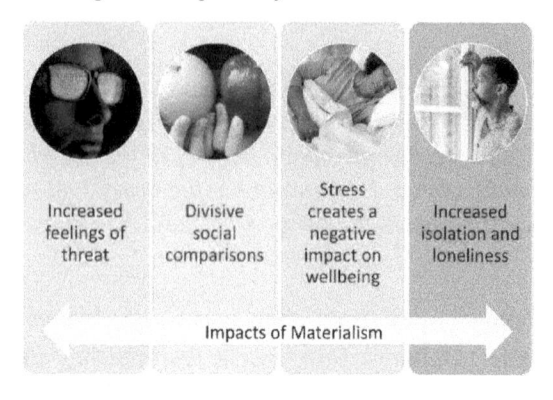

- Increased feelings of threat
- Divisive social comparisons
- Stress creates a negative impact on wellbeing
- Increased isolation and loneliness

Impacts of Materialism

Increasing feelings of threat: Materialism has been linked to increased aggression, particularly when individuals perceive their material possessions, status or self-image as being threatened. The emphasis on acquiring and protecting material goods can lead to competitive and aggressive behaviours as people strive to maintain or enhance their status. This competitive nature can escalate to violence, especially in environments where resources are scarce or highly valued.

Exacerbating social comparison: When individuals constantly compare their material wealth to others and perceive themselves as lacking, they may experience frustration and resentment. This emotional response is particularly true in consumer-driven societies where material success is often equated with personal worth.

Impacting on wellbeing: Materialism is also associated with lower wellbeing and life satisfaction, which can contribute to negative emotional states such as depression and anger. These emotional states can, in turn, increase the likelihood of violent behaviour, as individuals may lash out in response to their feelings of inadequacy or frustration.

Isolation and loneliness: As there is a greater shift towards individualism, our community supports begin to suffer. Approximately one in six Australians is experiencing emotional loneliness, one in ten lacks social support[84]. This disconnection from the community is not only a result of the individual isolation noted above but also is a key risk factor for developing loneliness. It also removes the social accountability that may prevent internal distress from spilling over into self-harm (self-directed violence) or outward aggression.

The environment is also a victim of violence within materialistic cultures. When people prioritise purchases and possession of the latest trends, there are usually elevated levels of excess consumption. Production of the goods that people desire requires environmental resources, and with increased consumption comes increased environmental degradation.

"What consumerism really is, at its worst is getting people to buy things that don't actually improve their lives."
~ Jeff Bezos

The Impact of Economic Policy

Economic policy can significantly influence the levels of materialism within a society by shaping the cultural environment in which people live and the messaging they receive about what constitutes success. For example:

Promotion of consumer spending: Economic policies emphasising consumer spending as a key driver of economic growth can foster a culture of materialism. When economic success is measured by consumer spending, it can create a societal norm that equates material wealth with personal success and happiness.

Advertising and marketing: Governments may support industries that rely heavily on advertising and marketing, further promoting materialistic values. Policies that allow or encourage aggressive marketing practices can lead to a societal focus on acquiring the latest products, as individuals are constantly bombarded with messages that link material possessions to status, happiness, and success.

Widening economic disparities: Economic policies that lead to significant income inequality can exacerbate materialism as individuals become more focused on their relative economic status. When there is a large gap between the wealthy and the rest of the population, people may feel pressure to compete materially, leading to increased emphasis on acquiring wealth and possessions as a way to signal success. The desire to appear successful can encourage individuals to prioritise material gains over other values, such as community, relationships, or personal growth.

Privatisation of public goods: When economic policies promote the privatisation of public goods and services, it can shift values from collective wellbeing to individual wealth accumulation. This shift can encourage materialism as individuals become more focused on securing personal financial resources to access previously publicly provided services, such as healthcare, education, and housing.

Materialism Makes it Harder to Tackle Violence

Materialism, the relationship between possessions and self-identity, has become mainstream in our society. This cultural trend spells danger for our ability to reduce violence. A recent study found a direct and positive association between materialism and aggressive behaviour and an indirect decrease in prosocial behaviour through the mediator of empathy[85]. Individuals who placed a high value on material possessions were more likely to exhibit aggressive tendencies. This link suggests that materialistic individuals may use aggression as a means to acquire or protect material wealth and status.

Some studies have shown that the individualistic views associated with materialism increase aggression due to a reduced ability to enact self-restraint. For example, research comparing individualistic and collectivistic cultures has shown that people in collectivistic societies, which emphasise group goals and conformity, often exhibit higher self-control, maintaining group harmony and adherence to social expectations. In contrast, individualistic cultures may encourage behaviours that prioritise personal desires, sometimes at the expense of self-restraint. This occurs due to the materialistic values eroding empathy for the situation and struggles of others.

Materialism can promote a culture of dehumanisation, and the absence of empathy means there are fewer inhibitors to undertaking all forms of physical and psychological violence. Moreover, it can lessen the effectiveness of reparative responses when violence occurs for without a sense of compassion for the victim, the perpetrator is unlikely to develop a sense of personal responsibility and be committed to behaviour change.

Core Concepts

Materialistic individuals believe that tangible possessions are not only symbols of success but also crucial to self-identity and social status.

Materialism has become a mainstream value in Australia.

Materialism is linked to:

- Higher levels of aggression.
- Lower levels of behavioural self-restraint.
- Reduced levels of empathy.

These consequences not only increase the level of aggression in society but make restorative and reparative treatments less effective.

Economic policy encourages materialism through the following:

- Promotion of consumer spending as a measure of success.
- Advertising and marketing policies.
- Increases in inequality.
- Privatisation of public goods.

14. How the Family Court May Exacerbate Violence

The Australian Family Court plays a crucial role in resolving disputes related to separation, custody, and the division of assets. However, the intense emotional and financial pressures involved in these proceedings can sometimes exacerbate tensions, leading to the escalation of conflict and, in some cases, violence. As families navigate the complexities of custody battles and divorce settlements, the threat of losing children or financial resources can push individuals to desperate and extreme actions.

The Threat of Loss

We have seen over and again that many people who perpetrate violence feel threatened in some way. Violence, be it physical or psychological, becomes a way to solve the problem of feeling vulnerable, to protect themselves from what they see as peril from other people. If there is one situation where people will become afraid for their future, it is with the threat of losing their financial assets or their family.

It is important to note that this threat does not just occur within the confines of the Family Court system. It can begin long before with one partner applying psychological violence through verbal threats or emotional manipulation to suggest that the other will lose in any forthcoming legal fight. The adversarial process begins long before the couple is in court and can promulgate frustration and fear. In this way, one partner can use potential outcomes from the court process as a form of coercive control.

Even if one partner is not using a potential court process to gain an advantage, the belief in negative outcomes from separation can occur from stories heard from friends, family and in the media. Reports of people who have lost everything through divorce and custody proceedings would weigh heavily on the minds of those facing the same process and lead to a sense of helplessness. Beliefs shape our reality, and so if a person thinks that they will inevitably suffer loss through the Family Court process, then this will automatically create a significant source of stress that may increase violent impulses.

Promoting Psychological Violence

It can be argued that the adversarial nature of the family court system can be seen to support psychological violence. It encourages partners to present evidence against each other with faults, failures, or negative behaviours of the opposing party used to secure favourable outcomes. The need to seem superior to the opposing party could involve:

- Making exaggerated or false accusations.
- Using children as pawns in disputes.
- Threatening financial ruin.

Such tactics are meant to destabilise the other party emotionally, coercing them into a settlement or agreement out of fear or exhaustion. The adversarial system can thus perpetuate cycles of emotional abuse, especially when one party uses the legal process as a tool of control.

Moreover, the adversarial nature of family court often reinforces negative beliefs and attitudes. Rather than fostering reconciliation or healing, the system encourages each party to view the other as an adversary, potentially leading to feelings of hatred, resentment, and revenge. These negative emotions can perpetuate psychological violence long after the legal proceedings have ended. This lingering emotional turmoil can affect not only the individuals involved but also their children and extended families.

The Psychological Impact of Custody Battles

Custody battles are among the most emotionally charged disputes that occur in the family court system. The stakes are extraordinarily high, as parents not only face the potential loss of their children but also the fear of being labelled as unfit or inferior. The psychological toll that custody disputes can take on parents is profound and multifaceted, often leading to emotional distress, anxiety, depression, and even violent behaviour.

The Fear of Losing Children

One of the most significant psychological impacts of custody battles is the intense fear of losing one's children. This fear is deeply rooted in the parental instinct to protect and care for one's offspring, and the prospect of losing custody can feel like an existential threat. Research has shown that this fear can lead to severe psychological distress, manifesting as anxiety, depression, and panic attacks[86]. For many parents, the thought of being separated from their children is unbearable, leading to extreme emotional reactions and, in some cases, desperate actions.

When parents feel that their relationship with their children is threatened, they may resort to extreme measures to protect their parental rights. Such responses can include verbal threats, harassment, or even physical violence against the other parent[87]. The fear and desperation that accompany the potential loss of one's children can push individuals to act in ways they might not otherwise consider, leading to dangerous and destructive outcomes.

The Fear of Being Seen as Unfit

This fear is often exacerbated by the adversarial nature of the court proceedings, where parents must present themselves in the best possible light while simultaneously discrediting the other parent. The pressure to "win" the custody battle can lead to heightened stress levels and a sense of constant vigilance, as parents fear making any mistake that could be used against them in court[88]. This relentless pressure can contribute to a decline in mental health, making it difficult for parents to function effectively in their daily lives. For those parties with an unrealistic sense of self-esteem, such a challenge to their sense of identity may become unbearable and incite violent impulses, putting them in a position of attack.

The Emotional Strain of Litigation

Litigation itself is a process that can take months or even years, during which time the psychological toll on parents can be immense. The prolonged uncertainty and the adversarial nature of the process can lead to chronic stress, which has been linked to a range of mental health issues, including anxiety disorders, depression, and even post-traumatic stress disorder (PTSD). The ongoing legal battle often prevents parents from moving on with their lives, trapping them in a cycle of conflict and emotional turmoil. The adversarial system encourages parents to gather evidence against one another, often involving their children in the process. When children are involved, this can exacerbate feelings of guilt and inadequacy, as parents may feel that they are failing their children by subjecting them to such a hostile environment.

The psychological impact of custody battles is not limited to the parents alone; it also extends to the children involved. Research has consistently shown that children who are caught in the middle of high-conflict custody disputes are at increased risk for a range of emotional and behavioural problems, including anxiety, depression, and difficulties in school[89]. In this way, the family court system may be creating intergenerational trauma and systems of maladaptive behaviours.

Financial Stress and the Risk of Violence

Divorce and separation often bring significant financial strain, which can exacerbate existing tensions and, in some cases, lead to violence. The division of assets, the negotiation of spousal and child support, and the potential for financial instability are all factors that contribute to the emotional and psychological stress experienced during these processes. When financial resources are perceived to be under threat, individuals may resort to desperate measures, including violence, to protect their interests.

Research has shown that financial stress is a significant predictor of both physical and psychological violence in relationships. Studies have found that financial strain was associated with an increased risk of intimate partner violence, particularly when one partner felt that their financial security was being threatened[90]. The pressure to maintain financial stability can push individuals to engage in aggressive or controlling behaviours to protect their economic interests.

It has also been shown that individuals who experience a significant decline in their financial status after divorce are also more likely to engage in aggressive or violent behaviour as they struggle to cope with the stress and insecurity of their new financial reality and diminished quality of lifestyle. The division of assets can lead to significant financial disadvantage, resentment and conflict, particularly if the financial settlement is perceived as unfair.

Psychological violence can also become a part of legal proceedings where an abuser may use financial leverage to exert power and control over the other party. For example, an individual might withhold financial support, delay the sale of shared assets, or hide assets to limit the other party's financial independence. This manipulation can create a power imbalance that exacerbates the distress of the victim, making them more vulnerable to coercion and potentially increasing the risk of violence. The stress and fear associated with financial insecurity can lead to a situation where the victim feels trapped and unable to escape the abusive relationship, further escalating the potential for violence[91].

Research also highlights that financial stress can exacerbate pre-existing mental health issues, leading to a higher risk of aggression and violence in high-conflict separation cases[92].

The Harm Has Been Recognised

"Adversarial systems do not work when we're talking about safety and they do not work when we're talking about the wellbeing of children," ~ Angharad Candlin

In 2017, a Committee of the Australian Parliament adopted an inquiry into how Australia's federal family law system can better support and protect people affected by family violence. This inquiry recognised and reported on several of the above issues, including that:

- The adversarial system is inappropriate for resolving family law disputes.
- It is open to abuse of process, including ongoing coercion and control of victims.
- It does not respond sufficiently to perjury and false allegations[93].

The Family Violence Working Group (FVWG) comprises senior justice officials from various Australian jurisdictions. It has continued the work of the 2017 Inquiry, focusing on improving the legal response to family violence[94].

To date, it has implemented the following initiatives:

The Lighthouse Project: This initiative involves early risk screening, triage, and tailored case management for family law cases involving family violence. It aims to identify and respond to safety concerns more effectively, ensuring that high-risk cases receive the attention and resources needed to protect vulnerable individuals.

Family Law Amendment Act 2023: This amendment enhances protections against family violence, including specific provisions for coercive control. It removes the presumption of equal shared parental responsibility in cases involving family violence, prioritising the safety and wellbeing of children.

Better support for children and families: The initiative aims to ensure that children's safety is prioritised in family law matters, with measures designed to protect them from exposure to family violence. It emphasises the importance of child-focused legal processes.

Training for legal professionals: This initiative provides specialised training for legal professionals to improve their handling of family violence cases. The training is designed to enhance their understanding of family violence dynamics and ensure they are better equipped to support victims and manage cases effectively.

Consistency across jurisdictions: Improving information sharing between agencies and developing consistent approaches across the country's multiple family law systems.

A set of guiding principles for protecting vulnerable witnesses in family violence and family law proceedings for use in all jurisdictions.

Ongoing Work to Reduce Harm

However, there is more work to be done. Recommendations raised for further improvements to reduce harm include:

Increased use of mediation as an alternative to adversarial court proceedings. Mediation allows parties to resolve disputes more collaboratively and less confrontational, reducing the likelihood of escalating conflict.

Better support for families during separation. Providing better support for families going through divorce is essential in reducing the stress and conflict that can lead to violence.

This support may include offering access to counselling, financial advice, and parenting support services.

The family court system must be more attuned to the risks of violence (physical and psychological) in separation and custody cases. Increasing awareness of risk includes recognising the potential for financial stress, custody battles, and adversarial legal processes to exacerbate existing tensions and lead to violent outcomes.

Integrating psychological support services within the family law system is essential for helping parties manage the emotional toll of custody and divorce disputes. Offering access to mental health professionals, such as psychologists or counsellors, can provide individuals with the tools they need to cope with the stress and anxiety associated with legal proceedings.

Core Concepts

The intense emotional and financial pressures involved in Family Court cases can sometimes exacerbate tensions, leading to the escalation of conflict and violence.

The threat of court proceedings and their outcomes can be used as a form of psychological violence aimed at securing power.

The adversarial nature of the Family Court system may encourage psychological violence as it pushes partners to present evidence against each other with faults, failures, or negative behaviours of the opposing party used to secure favourable outcomes.

In custody battles, parents not only face the potential loss of their children but also the fear of being labelled as unfit or inferior.

When parents feel that their relationship with their children is under threat, they may resort to extreme measures in an attempt to protect their parental rights.

Financial stress is a significant predictor of both physical and psychological violence in relationships, particularly when one partner feels that their financial security is being threatened.

Psychological violence can also become a part of legal proceedings where an abuser may use financial leverage to exert power and control over the other party.

15. Case Studies

Change is possible, and some communities are successfully reducing the prevalence and impact of violence. Here are three examples of where a dedicated and holistic approach to understanding and treating all forms of violence is bringing positive results.

Scotland's Violence Reduction Unit: A Model for Reducing Violence

Scotland's Violence Reduction Unit (VRU)[95] has become a global example of how to successfully tackle violence through innovative, community-based approaches. Established in 2005, the VRU has transformed the way Scotland addresses violent crime, particularly knife crime, by treating violence as a public health issue rather than solely a criminal justice problem. The VRU's multifaceted strategies, including education, rehabilitation, community engagement, and policy reform, have significantly reduced violence and transformed lives.

The VRU was formed in response to Scotland's alarming rates of violent crime, which had earned Glasgow the reputation of being the "murder capital" of Europe. At the time, knife crime and gang violence were rampant, particularly among young men in deprived areas. Recognising the limitations of traditional policing methods, the VRU adopted a public health approach, viewing violence as a preventable disease that could be treated through early intervention, education, and community support.

The VRU's approach is rooted in prevention and rehabilitation, focusing on addressing the root causes of violence rather than merely reacting to incidents. Some of the key strategies implemented by the VRU include:

Education and Awareness: The VRU strongly emphasises educating young people about the dangers of violence. Programs such as the "No Knives, Better Lives" initiative aim to change attitudes toward knife carrying and violence through school-based education, peer mentoring, and community engagement.

Gang Intervention and Support: One of the VRU's most successful initiatives has been its work with gang members. The unit employs former gang members as mentors who work directly with young people involved in gangs, offering them support and alternatives to violent lifestyles. This approach has been instrumental in reducing gang-related violence.

Mentorship and Role Models: The VRU partners with local communities to provide mentorship programs where young people are paired with positive role models who guide them away from violence and towards constructive activities, such as sports, arts, and vocational training.

Community Engagement and Empowerment: The VRU works closely with local communities to empower residents to actively prevent violence. Initiatives include supporting community-led initiatives and providing resources for local projects that promote safety and cohesion.

Support for Victims and Offenders: Recognising that many offenders are also victims of violence or adverse circumstances, the VRU offers support services that address trauma, mental health issues, and social inequalities. By providing holistic support, the VRU helps individuals break the cycle of violence and reintegrate into society.

Since its inception, the VRU has profoundly impacted reducing violence in Scotland. Knife crime, which was once endemic in cities like Glasgow, has seen a dramatic decrease, with youth violence reduced by more than 50 per cent in some areas. The success of the VRU can be attributed to its comprehensive approach, which addresses the social determinants of violence and engages communities in the process of change.

The VRU's work has reduced crime and changed the culture around violence in Scotland. Where once carrying a knife was seen as a sign of toughness, there is now a growing recognition of the devastating impact of violence on individuals and communities. The VRU has helped shift public attitudes, making Scotland safer and more resilient.

The VRU's success has drawn international attention, and the model has been studied and replicated in other countries facing similar challenges. The unit's work has demonstrated that violence can be significantly reduced when it is treated as a public health issue, with a focus on prevention, early intervention, and community support.

Key lessons from the Violence Reduction Unit's approach include the following:

- Establishment of a centralised authority that coordinates messages and develops consistent responses.
- Treatment of violence as a public health issue rather than solely a criminal justice problem.
- Support for both victims and offenders.
- A holistic view of violence in both its physical and psychological forms.
- Recognition of the role that societal inequality plays in violence.
- Importance of multi-agency collaboration.
- The need for long-term investment in prevention programs.
- The value in engaging communities in the process of change.

Iceland's Youth Substance Use Prevention Program

Substance use can be understood as a form of self-directed violence because it involves intentionally engaging in behaviours that are harmful to one's health and wellbeing. When individuals use substances such as alcohol, drugs, or even excessive amounts of legal substances like caffeine, they may be seeking to escape emotional pain, stress, or trauma. However, these substances can cause significant physical and psychological harm, including addiction, mental health disorders, and physical health problems. This self-destructive behaviour can be seen as a way of inflicting harm on oneself, either consciously or subconsciously.

Iceland's Youth Substance Use Prevention Program[96] has emerged as one of the most effective public health initiatives in the world. This program, which began in the late 1990s, successfully reduced substance abuse and, thus, self-harm among teenagers to remarkably low levels. It transformed Iceland from having one of the highest rates of teenage substance use in Europe to one of the lowest. The program's success is attributed to a comprehensive, community-based approach that engages families, schools, and local governments in creating a supportive environment for youth.

In the 1990s, Iceland faced a significant public health crisis with high rates of alcohol, tobacco, and drug use among its youth. Surveys showed that 42 per cent of Icelandic teenagers had been drunk in the past month, and many were engaging in regular smoking and drug use. Urgent action was needed, so Icelandic authorities launched the Youth Substance Use Prevention Program in collaboration with researchers and policymakers.

The program was based on extensive research that identified key factors contributing to substance abuse, including a lack of structured activities, weak family ties, and inadequate community support. With this understanding, the program sought to address these root causes by fostering a supportive environment that would promote healthy behaviours and reduce the appeal of substance use.

The success of Iceland's program is largely due to its multifaceted approach, which focuses on several key areas:

Parental Engagement: One of the cornerstones of the program is the emphasis on strengthening parental involvement in their children's lives. Parents were encouraged to spend more time with their children, know their friends, and set clear rules regarding alcohol and drug use. The program also introduced agreements among parents to limit unsupervised time and establish curfews, ensuring that teenagers spent more time at home or in supervised activities.

Extracurricular Activities: Recognising that boredom and lack of structure were major risk factors for substance use, the program greatly expanded the availability of extracurricular activities for teenagers. The government provided substantial funding to sports clubs, music schools, art programs, and other extracurricular activities, making them affordable and accessible to all youth. These gave teenagers positive outlets for their energy and creativity, reducing the likelihood of them turning to substance use.

Community and School Collaboration: The program fostered close collaboration between schools, local governments, and community organisations. Schools played a vital role in educating students about the dangers of substance use and promoting healthy lifestyles. At the same time, community organisations provided additional support through youth centres and after-school programs. This collective effort ensured that teenagers received consistent messages about the importance of staying substance-free.

Surveys and Data-Driven Policy: From the outset, the program relied heavily on data to guide its strategies. Annual surveys were conducted to monitor substance use among teenagers, allowing authorities to track progress and make adjustments as needed. This data-driven approach ensured that the program remained effective and responsive to emerging trends.

Legal and Policy Measures: Iceland also implemented strict legal measures to support the program's goals. The legal drinking age was raised to twenty, and the government imposed heavy restrictions on the sale and advertising of alcohol and tobacco. These measures, combined with the program's broader initiatives, created an environment where substance use became increasingly difficult and less socially acceptable.

The results of Iceland's Youth Substance Use Prevention Program have been nothing short of extraordinary. Over the past two decades, the country has seen a dramatic decline in youth substance use. By 2016, the percentage of 15- and 16-year-olds who had been drunk in the past month had dropped from 42 per cent to just 5 per cent. Similarly, the rates of daily smoking among teenagers fell from 23 per cent to 3 per cent, and drug use declined significantly.

These achievements have made Iceland a global leader in youth substance use prevention. The program's success has been recognised internationally, and its model has been studied and adapted by other countries seeking to address similar public health challenges.

The success of Iceland's Youth Substance Use Prevention Program offers valuable lessons for other countries and communities facing similar issues. The program's holistic approach—focusing on parental involvement, structured activities, community engagement, and data-driven policy—demonstrates the importance of addressing the root causes of substance use and self-harm rather than just its symptoms.

Key takeaways from Iceland's experience include the:
- Need for strong collaboration between families, schools, and communities.

- Creation of a supportive environment that fosters healthy development.
- Message that this program sends that the community cares for their youth.
- Need to identify and address the root causes of the problem.
- Benefit of treating the situation as a public health issue rather than as youth recalcitrance.
- Importance of providing positive and attractive alternatives to substance use and self-harm to solve problems.
- Value of using data to inform and adapt policies.

New Zealand's Family Violence Programs

New Zealand has long been recognised for its proactive and comprehensive approach to addressing family violence. The country's family violence programs[97] have been developed over decades, responding to the high rates of domestic violence and aiming to create safer communities. Through a combination of legal reforms, public awareness campaigns, and support services, New Zealand has made significant strides in reducing both the incidence and impact of family violence.

New Zealand has historically faced challenges with high rates of family violence. The need for a coordinated and multifaceted response became evident as the consequences of domestic violence, including the impact on children and the economic burden on society, were increasingly recognised. In collaboration with non-governmental organisations (NGOs) and community groups, the New Zealand government developed a range of programs designed to address these issues at multiple levels, from prevention to intervention.

New Zealand's family violence programs are notable for their breadth and depth, incorporating legal, social, and educational components.

The "It's Not OK" Campaign

The "It's Not OK" campaign was launched in 2007 and is one of New Zealand's most visible and impactful public awareness initiatives. The campaign seeks to change attitudes and behaviours related to family violence, making it socially unacceptable. The campaign used mass media, community outreach, and personal stories to raise awareness about the signs of family violence and encourage bystander intervention. It emphasises that violence is not a private matter but a societal issue that requires collective action. The five strands of this campaign were:

Mass Media Advertising: Raising awareness and spreading key messages about family violence through television and other media, emphasising that violence is not acceptable and that it's important to seek and offer help.

Community Action and Capacity Building: Collaborating with communities to develop their own campaigns, providing financial support, resources, and training to empower local change agents. Partnerships with national organisations also help build an informal support network.

Champions of Change: Engaging men who have overcome their past violent behaviours to share their stories and challenge harmful beliefs about masculinity, inspiring others to change.

Communications, Resources, and Tools: Creating and distributing educational materials, toolkits, and guidelines to promote behaviour change, supported by a comprehensive online presence.

Research and Evaluation: Researching to understand the factors influencing family violence, evaluate the campaign's effectiveness, and continuously refine strategies based on audience feedback.

The "It's Not OK" campaign has been credited with:
- Increasing public knowledge and awareness about family violence and understanding its impacts.
- Prompting people and communities to reconsider their attitudes and beliefs towards family violence.
- Behaviour change, including reducing the stigma around help-seeking and help-giving behaviours.
- Beginning to shift some community and societal attitudes and norms, including:
    - Beliefs that change is possible.
    - Reducing tolerance of violence.
- Fostering greater community involvement in preventing family violence.

Specialist Family Violence Courts

Recognising that the legal system plays a crucial role in addressing family violence, New Zealand has established Specialist Family Violence Courts. These courts are designed to handle cases of family violence with greater expertise and sensitivity. These courts focus on swift intervention and provide access to support services for both victims and perpetrators. Judges and court staff receive specialised training to handle family violence cases, ensuring that victims receive the protection and support they need while offenders are held accountable in a way that encourages rehabilitation. The establishment of these courts has led to faster processing of family violence cases and has provided a more supportive environment for victims. The specialised approach has also contributed to better outcomes in reducing repeat offences.

Whānau Ora Initiative

The Whānau Ora initiative is a Māori-led approach to improving the wellbeing of families, recognising that family violence often intersects with broader issues such as poverty, health, and education. Whānau Ora provides holistic support to families, addressing the underlying causes of family violence through culturally appropriate services. The initiative empowers families to develop their own solutions to the challenges they face, with the support of community organisations and government agencies. Whānau Ora has been effective in reaching communities that may not engage with mainstream services, particularly Māori and Pacific Islander families. By addressing the root causes of violence and focusing on overall wellbeing, the initiative has helped reduce the incidence of family violence in these communities.

Police and Community Collaboration

The New Zealand Police have taken an active role in addressing family violence, working closely with community organisations to provide a coordinated response. The police have established Family Violence Teams, which include specially trained officers who respond to incidents of family violence. These teams work with community organisations to provide immediate support to victims and ensure that offenders are referred to appropriate services for rehabilitation. The collaboration between police and community organisations has led to more effective interventions, with a focus on preventing further violence and supporting victims. This approach has also improved the police's ability to identify and respond to family violence cases.

The comprehensive nature of New Zealand's family violence programs has led to measurable improvements in reducing domestic violence. Public awareness of family violence has increased, and more victims are seeking help. The introduction of Specialist Family Violence Courts and the Whānau Ora initiative has provided targeted support to those most in need, resulting in better protection for victims and more effective rehabilitation for offenders. New Zealand's approach has also served as a model for other countries looking to develop their own strategies for reducing family violence.

The success of these programs underscores the importance of:

A Holistic Approach: Addressing both the immediate and underlying causes of family violence, including social, economic, and cultural factors.

Community Engagement: Involving community organisations and culturally relevant initiatives like Whānau Ora to reach diverse populations effectively.

Specialised Legal Interventions: Establishing specialised courts and train legal professionals to handle family violence cases with greater sensitivity and expertise.

Consistent Mass Media Messaging: Implementing sustained public awareness campaigns to change societal attitudes towards family violence.

Collaboration: Fostering strong collaboration between police, social services, and community organisations for a coordinated response to family violence.

Evidence-Based Decision Making: Continually improving the understanding of the drivers of violence and the effectiveness of interventions.

16. A Personal Pathway

Violence is often seen as something that exists outside of us, perpetuated by "bad people" in situations that seem far away from our everyday lives. However, the truth is that violence can touch us in ways that we might not immediately recognise. Whether through our own actions or words, through what we watch or by simply standing by, violence can be a regular part of our worlds.

The following diagram invites you to take a personal journey of reflection, asking honest questions about where violence may be present in your own life and exploring where you would like to make a change.

This exercise is all about awareness - asking yourself the hard questions and responding with courage, and moreover identifying and creating space for action. Let this be a pathway that may guide you towards understanding and towards greater personal power.

Understanding My Beliefs
What do I believe about violence?   • What it is.   • Who does it.   • Why it occurs.   Are any of these beliefs faulty or not supported with facts?

Do I believe violence is justified? If so, when?

Do I believe I can be violent?

Would others say that I can be violent?

Understanding My Emotions and Behaviours

When have I been violent – either physically or psychologically?

How do I react when I feel threatened in some way?

What do I do when I get angry?

How do I find pride operating in my life?

Do I condone violence conducted by others? Why?

How do I process shame and guilt?

Am I influenced by materialistic values? If so, how does this impact my wellbeing?

Understanding My Environment

Where am I exposed to violence in my environment?

Where am I exposed to violence in the entertainment I choose?

Have I become desensitised to harmful words and actions I see around me?

Where are there systemic forms of violence in my community (for example, inequality, discrimination, racism, poverty)?

Actions I Can Take

Are there any action I need to take to become more aware about violence and how it plays out in my life?

Are there any skills I could build to help me deal with anger, pride, shame and guilt?

Do I need to build or strengthen my support systems to help me deal with stress and manage harmful habits?

Would it be helpful to share what I have learnt in this book with others to build better communication and connections?

17. A Political Pathway

Violence doesn't just unfold on the streets or behind closed doors—it's also embedded within the policies and practices that shape our communities. This chapter asks all decision-makers to reflect on how violence might be woven into their portfolios, decisions, and even their own workplaces.

By questioning beliefs about violence and examining its subtle presence in their spheres of influence, leaders can begin to identify opportunities for change. This is an invitation to critically assess not just what policies are implemented, but also the culture in which they operate.

It is also a reminder that those in the hallways of power are themselves role models and so must make sure they are taking actions against violence at the same time they are asking their people to do the same. Let this be a pathway to a holistic and helpful approach to violence within your own walls as well as across the societies which you govern.

Understanding My Beliefs
What do I believe about violence?   • What it is.   • Who does it.   • Why it occurs.   Are any of these beliefs faulty or not supported with facts?

Do I believe certain types of violence are justified or necessary in governance?

Are there any policies or systems I oversee that sustain systematic violence?

Understanding My Emotions and Behaviours

In what ways might my actions or decisions contribute to institutional or systemic violence?

How do I respond to criticism or opposition?

Do I condone aggressive tactics in political discourse or policy enforcement?

Have my policies or decisions led to unintended harm?

Do the systems I oversee create feelings of shame or use adversarial approaches to determine outcomes?

Understanding My Environment

How prevalent is violence within my workplace or the political environment I operate within?

Does the political culture around me normalise verbal violence, aggressive rhetoric or bullying?

Have I become desensitised to the systematic violence occurring within the community (inequality, discrimination, racism, poverty, sexism).

Do I have a holistic view of all the places violence shows up within the societies I lead?

Do I see any inconsistencies in approaches to violence across different portfolios (for example, media, sport, justice, health)?

Actions I Can Take

Are there any action I need to take to become more aware about violence and how it plays across my community?

What steps could I take to understand how violence could be embedded in my policies or portfolio?

Do I need to build or strengthen support systems that foster non-violent political discourse?

> Are there opportunities to learn or advocate for non-violent approaches to problem solving within my role?
>
> Would it be helpful to share what I have learnt in this book with colleagues to bring greater clarity and consistency in our understanding of and approaches to violence?

Conclusion

Knowledge ≠Power.
Knowledge + Action = Power.

Violence is a behaviour and chosen, either consciously or unconsciously by a person to solve a situation in which they feel powerless. Very few people cause harm simply for the pleasure of inflicting pain. For the majority it is a way to solve a problem, often which is a sense of great vulnerability. Violence is a response to a feeling of threat. People lash out when they fear for their physical health, the loss of valuable resources, their social status or sense of identity. Violence is chosen because it has become a habit, part of their ingrained identity, or the person has no skills or faith in the alternatives.

Violent in Different Ways

While, rightly, much attention is being placed upon the physical violence being perpetrated by men, we must remember that women too are violent, just in different ways. Women and girls use verbal violence, social and emotional manipulation to achieve harmful ends, and the human toll they exact is very real. Both genders are dealing with thousands of years of ingrained identities and automatic responses to assert power and solve problems.

Systemic Violence and Self-Harm

There are two types of violence that struck me as I was writing this book that I would like to stress again before its end. The first is systemic violence. All forms of discrimination and inequality are a form of violence, for they deprive people of their ability to live to their fullest potential. Ultimately, they are born from decisions made by those in power and result in trapping people in states of distress and despair. Additionally, toxic work cultures that allow or even enable a lack of psychological safety must be seen also as communities in which violence has become the norm.

The second is what we know in Australia as self-harm, or which the United Nations calls self-directed violence. Here, people feel powerless, but choose to inflict suffering on themselves. When we consider self-harm in all its forms, including causing physical injury and substance abuse, we see a bigger picture of violence in our communities. It is not just a behaviour that is targeted towards others. When people feel threatened in some way, when they cannot adequately deal with the distress they are experiencing, they can also choose to cause suffering to themselves.

The Danger of Desensitisation

Violence is an individual behaviour, but can be seen as a viable solution because it is supported, directly or indirectly by the situations and societies in which the person lives. Writing this book, I was astounded by how areas of my life violence can be found and how much I had become desensitised to it. Whether it be at work, on TV or hearing a new release song on the radio, the extent of harm being presented and publicised is alarming. There are so many subtle cues influencing our views on violence, and normalising the idea of harm as a means to entertain and to excel.

Comprehensive and Consistent Policies

This experience has made me more determined than ever to encourage a consistent and holistic understanding of violence, especially for policymakers. For some politicians are violent too, because they are also people, and like everyone else, at times they feel afraid. Yet, these are the people we need to be courageous in implementing policies and practices to shift harmful beliefs about violence.

It is absolutely critical that action is taken to address the tragic occurrences of family and domestic violence in this country. In addition, though, I do believe that we need to have a comprehensive view about violence in our society. We must see violence in all its forms and seek to change the beliefs and behaviours that underlie all of its manifestations. Where violence in sport, news, entertainment, politics or porn is excused, ignored or condoned, then confusion and hypocrisy will dilute attempts to reduce harm in other areas. Moreover, the policies and practices implemented to reduce violence must be founded on love - the aim to reduce suffering and allow all to achieve their highest potential. Fear based strategies do not work, for they only fuel the flames of threat and anger that lead to aggression.

Personal Responsibility

However, while we can look to governments to make change, ultimately, it begins with individuals, each of us.

"Be the change that you wish to see in the world." ~
Mahatma Gandhi

This book has been a journey of self-discovery, uncovering and challenging the assumptions I held about violence in my life and the society in which I live. I have learnt so much, and this has led me to several personal conclusions.

I Am Violent

Following in the courageous footsteps of Mark Kulkens, I am now able to understand that I there are many ways in which I may be perpetrating violence. Not physically, but potentially psychologically. And not always intentionally, but still with the possibility to be harmful. Remembering that violence is in the eye of the receiver, there could be times that my passionate speech has been felt as an aggressive attack, or my generalised frustration has been received as a personal assault. I too need to take greater responsibility for how my behaviours may affect others.

I Condone Violence

I watch it and enjoy it. Be it the bitchy bullying on the Reality TV shows, the biff in the action movies or the gruesome murders on true crime series, the drama of other people's interactions is interesting. In my own workplace there are those who inflict psychological harm on others every day under the guise of "reasonable management action", and yet I do not call this out for what it is. However, now I realise more than ever that:

"Victims of violence depend on bystanders to bear witness to what is happening and take a stand against it. It is the only way". ~ Roy F. Baumeister

Where I don't, I am enabling the continued perpetration of violent behaviour.

I Can Be Courageous

Writing this book has shown me that with a clear intention and dedicated action, I can understand and challenge my beliefs and behaviours. I can be brave enough to seek information on issues that are tough and continue to learn every day.

I Can Make Change

I have the ability to seek support, shift my attitudes and assumptions so that my own life and the lives of those around me are better. I can shed light on my hypocrisies and with curiosity and compassion, I can make positive change. And while I do not have the answers, I can start conversations that may bring a more conscious and connected approach to helping others begin their own journeys away from violence.

Just One Drop

> *"Individually, we are one drop. Together, we are an ocean."*
> ~Ryūnosuke Satoro

This book is just one tiny contribution to the great work being done across communities to reduce the amount of violence. While I hope that it aids in some greater understanding, it is just one drop in a big ocean of conversations we need to have. It is a small voice in a large choir calling for action and a tiny push for each of us to examine our roles in both perpetuating and preventing violence. I acknowledge that this book may not do much by itself, but by helping me understand violence better, it has made an impact in my world.

Violence is a complex and challenging problem. It is an individual issue, a community challenge, a criminal justice dilemma, and a public health crisis all at once. There is no simple solution; this book only scratches the surface of its deep nature and the breadth of ways it manifests in our society. Yet, I hope it advances understanding, improves knowledge, and encourages people to make changes to keep themselves and their families safe.

Why? Because all deserve to live peaceful lives.

Please remember:
You deserve peace, and so do all of those around you.
There are better ways than violence to solve your problems.
There are people to help.
And seeking help is an act of bravery.
You can make a change.

Support and Advocacy Groups

1800RESPECT
Phone: 1800 737 732
Website: 1800respect.org.au
National helpline offering support for violence.

Lifeline Australia
Phone: 13 11 14
Website: lifeline.org.au
24/7 crisis support and suicide prevention service.

Salvation Army Australia
Phone: 13 SALVOS (13 72 58)
Website: salvationarmy.org.au
Provides support for victims of violence.

White Ribbon Australia
Email: contact@whiteribbon.org.au
Website: whiteribbon.org.au
Movement to end men's violence against women.

Beyond Blue
Phone: 1300 22 4636
Website: beyondblue.org.au
Support for mental health issues.

No to Violence

Phone: 1300 766 491

Website: ntv.org.au

Offers support for men including counselling.

The Centre for Nonviolent Communication

www.cnvc.org

An international nonprofit that helps people peacefully and effectively resolve conflicts.

About the Author

Belinda Tobin is a researcher, author, producer, and avid explorer of the human experience, with all its challenges and complexities. Her works span fiction, non-fiction, poetry, TV series and film. However, they all share a common purpose, to foster a more conscious, compassionate, courageous and connected future.

Find out more about Belinda and her projects at www.belindatobin.com.

References

[1] Violence. (2023, June 7). UNDRRwww.undrr.org/terminology/disaster-risk.

[2] Krug EG et al., eds. World report on violence and health. Geneva, World Health Organization, 2002.

[3] What is bullying? (n.d.). Australian Human Rights Commission. https://humanrights.gov.au/our-work/commission-general/what-bullying

[4] Feldman Barrett, L. (2017, July 14). When Is Speech Violence? The New York Times. https://www.nytimes.com/2017/07/14/opinion/sunday/when-is-speech-violence.html

[5] Suicide and intentional self-harm. (2024, February 14). Australian Institute of Health and Welfare. https://www.aihw.gov.au/suicide-self-harm-monitoring/summary/suicide-and-intentional-self-harm

[6] Rioseco, S. T. a. P. (n.d.). Self-injury among adolescents. https://growingupinaustralia.gov.au/research-findings/snapshots/self-injury-among-adolescents

[7] Bovell-Ammon BJ, Xuan Z, Paasche-Orlow MK, LaRochelle MR. Association of Incarceration With Mortality by Race From a National Longitudinal Cohort Study. JAMA Netw Open. 2021;4(12).

[8] Bovell-Ammon, B. J., Xuan, Z., Paasche-Orlow, M. K., & LaRochelle, M. R. (2021). Association of incarceration

with mortality by race from a national longitudinal cohort study. JAMA Network Open, 4(12), e2133083.

[9] Released prisoners returning to prison | Sentencing Council. (n.d.). www.sentencingcouncil.vic.gov.au/sentencing-statistics

[10] Galtung, Johan. "Violence, Peace, and Peace Research." Journal of Peace Research, vol. 6, no. 3, 1969, pp. 167–191

[11] Gilligan, James. "Preventing Violence." Thames & Hudson, 2001

[12] McCarthy KJ, Mehta R, Haberland NA (2018) Gender, power, and violence: A systematic review of measures and their association with male perpetration of IPV. PLoS ONE 13(11)

[13] Barrett, L. F. (2017). How Emotions Are Made: The Secret Life of the Brain. Houghton Mifflin Harcourt.

[14] Barrett, L. F. (2018). The science of emotions. In Healthy Living Made Simple (pp. 38–39).

[15] Connell, R. W., & Messerschmidt, J. W. (2005). Hegemonic Masculinity: Rethinking the Concept. Gender & Society, 19(6), 829-859.

[16] Reidy, D. E., Berke, D. S., Gentile, B., & Zeichner, A. (2014). Masculine Discrepancy Stress, Substance Use, Assault and Injury in a Survey of U.S. Men. Injury Prevention, 20(6), 400-404.

[17] OHCHR. (n.d.). Declaration on the Elimination of Violence against Women. https://www.ohchr.org/en/instruments-mechanisms/instruments/declaration-elimination-violence-against-women

[18] Crick, N. R., & Grotpeter, J. K. (1995). Relational Aggression, Gender, and Social-Psychological Adjustment. Child Development, 66(3), 710-722.

[19] Ridgeway, C. L., & Correll, S. J. (2004). Unpacking the Gender System: A Theoretical Perspective on Gender Beliefs and Social Relations. Gender & Society, 18(4), 510-531.

[20] Robinson, S. L., O'Reilly, J., & Wang, W. (2013). Workplace Ostracism: A Review of the Literature and Implications for Practice. Oxford Handbooks Online.

[21] Wright, M.F. (2020). The role of technologies, behaviors, gender, and gender stereotype traits in adolescents' cyber aggression. Journal of Interpersonal Violence, 35(7-8), 1719-1738.

[22] What is family and domestic violence - Family and domestic violence - Services Australia. (n.d.). https://www.servicesaustralia.gov.au

[23] Hausman, S. (2008, January 15). Aggression becoming more common in girls. NPR. https://www.npr.org/transcripts/18112648

[24] Huesmann LR. The impact of electronic media violence: scientific theory and research. J Adolesc Health. 2007 Dec;41(6 Suppl 1):S6-13.

[25] Bushman BJ, Huesmann LR. Effects of televised violence on aggression. In: Singer D, Singer J, editors. Handbook of children and the media. Thousand Oaks, CA: Sage Publications; 2001. pp. 223–54.

[26] Barker, M. J. (2018). The Psychology of Sex (The Psychology of Everything) (1st ed.). Routledge.

[27] Bridges, A. J., Wosnitzer, R., Scharrer, E., Sun, C., & Liberman, R. (2010). Aggression and Sexual Behavior in Best-Selling Pornography Videos: A Content Analysis Update. Violence Against Women, 16(10), 1065–1085.

[28] Havey, A., Puccio, D., & Thomas, K. S. (2017). Sex, Likes and Social Media: Talking to Our Teens in the Digital Age. Vermilion. Page 94.

[29] Lis, L. (2020). No Shame: Real Talk With Your Kids About Sex, Self-Confidence, and Healthy Relationships. Page 151.

[30] Lis, L. (2020). No Shame: Real Talk With Your Kids About Sex, Self-Confidence, and Healthy Relationships. Page 151.

[31] Havey, A., Puccio, D., & Thomas, K. S. (2017). Sex, Likes and Social Media: Talking to Our Teens in the Digital Age. Vermilion. Page 102.

[32] Havey, A., Puccio, D., & Thomas, K. S. (2017). Sex, Likes and Social Media: Talking to Our Teens in the Digital Age. Vermilion. Page 94.

[33] Dines, G. (2011). Portland: How Porn Has Hijacked Our Sexuality (1st ed.). Beacon Press. Page xxxiii.

[34] Quayle and Taylor, "Child Pornography and the Internet" as quoted in Dines, G. (2011). Portland: How Porn Has Hijacked Our Sexuality (1st ed.). Beacon Press. Page 159.

[35] Macdonald, H. (2018, June 22). Domestic violence spikes on State of Origin nights, study finds. ABC News. https://www.abc.net.au/news/2018-06-22/spike-in-domestic-violence-during-state-of-origin,-study-finds/9895684

[36] Lancaster University. (n.d.). World Cup football is a risk factor for domestic violence | Lancaster University. https://www.lancaster.ac.uk/news/articles/2013/world-cup-football-is-a-risk-factor-for-domestic-violence/

[37] Daignault I, Deslauriers-Varin N, Parent S. Profiles of Teenage Athletes' Exposure to Violence in Sport: An

Analysis of Their Sport Practice, Athletic Behaviors, and Mental Health. J Interpers Violence. 2023 Jun;38(11-12).

[38] Sorial, Sarah. "Seductive Violence: Parliamentary Debates and the Normalisation of Aggressive Political Rhetoric." Journal of Language and Politics, vol. 18, no. 6, 2019, pp. 804-823.

[39] Ilie, Cornelia. "Insulting as (Un)parliamentary Practice in the British and Swedish Parliaments: A Rhetorical Approach to the Study of Parliamentary Discourse." Journal of Pragmatics, vol. 41, no. 3, 2009, pp. 586-602.

[40] Grabe, Shelly, et al. "The Impact of Verbal Aggression in Politics: A Case Study of Psychological Effects on Politicians." Political Psychology, vol. 40, no. 2, 2020, pp. 285-303.

[41] Neria Y, Sullivan GM. (2011) "Understanding the mental health effects of indirect exposure to mass trauma through the media. JAMA. 2011 Sep 28;306(12):1374-5.

[42] Pickens, J. N., PhD. (2024, February 7). Viewing violent online images and videos is harmful. Psychology Today. https://www.psychologytoday.com/au/blog/psychology-through-technology/202402/traumatic-media-overload-could-impact-our-mental-health

[43] Gosselin, Denise K. Heavy Hands: An Introduction to the Crimes of Intimate and Family Violence. 5th ed., Prentice Hall, 2014.

[44] Baumeister, R. F. (2012). Human evil: The myth of pure evil and the true causes of violence. In M. Mikulincer & P. R. Shaver (Eds.), The social psychology of morality: Exploring the causes of good and evil (pp. 367–380). American Psychological Association.

[45] Barrett, L. F. (2017). How Emotions Are Made: The Secret Life of the Brain. Houghton Mifflin Harcourt.

[46] Baumeister, R. F. (2012). Human evil: The myth of pure evil and the true causes of violence. In M. Mikulincer & P. R. Shaver (Eds.), The social psychology of morality: Exploring the causes of good and evil (pp. 367–380). American Psychological Association.

[47] Kjærvik, S. L., & Bushman, B. J. (2021). The link between narcissism and aggression: A meta-analytic review. Psychological Bulletin, 147(5), 477–503.

[48] Galtung, J. (2018). Violence, peace and peace research. Organicom, 15(28), 33–56.

[49] Includes findings from Bushman, Brad & Coyne, Sarah & Anderson, Craig & Björkqvist, Kaj & Boxer, Paul & Dodge, Kenneth & Dubow, Eric & Farrington, David & Gentile, Douglas & Huesmann, L. & Lansford, Jennifer & Novaco, Raymond & Ostrov, Jamie & Underwood, Marion & Warburton, Wayne & Ybarra, Michele. (2018). Risk factors for youth violence: Youth Violence Commission, International Society For Research On Aggression (ISRA). Aggressive Behavior. 44. 331-336. 10.1002/ab.21766.

[50] Twenge, J. M., Baumeister, R. F., Tice, D. M., & Stucke, T. S. (2001). If you can't join them, beat them: Effects of social exclusion on aggressive behaviour. Journal of Personality and Social Psychology, 81(6), 1058-1069. DeWall, C. N., Deckman, T., Pond, R. S., & Bonser, I. (2011). Belongingness as a core personality trait: How social exclusion influences social functioning and creates a risk for violence. Personality and Social Psychology Review, 15(4), 274-290.

[51] Bushman, B. J., & Cooper, H. M. (1990). Effects of alcohol on human aggression: An intergrative research review. Psychological Bulletin, 107(3), 341–354.

[52] Kristjansson AL, Kogan SM, James JE, Sigfusdottir ID. Adolescent Caffeine Consumption and Aggressive Behavior: A Longitudinal Assessment. Substance Abuse. 2021;42(4):450-453.

[53] Hawkins, D. R. (1995). Power vs. Force: The Hidden Determinants of Human Behavior. Hay House.

[54] Martin, Colin, Preedy, Victor, R. and Patel, Vinood, B. (2023) Handbook of anger, aggression, and violence. Springer International, New York, USA. ISBN 9783031315466

[55] TenHouten, W.D., 2016a. Normlessness, anomie, and the emotions. Sociological Forum, 31 (2), 465–486.10.1111/socf.2016.31.issue-2

[56] Nathanson D (1992) Shame and pride: Affect, sex, and the birth of the self. New York: Norton

[57] Gilbert P. The evolution of social attractiveness and its role in shame, humiliation, guilt and therapy. Br J Med Psychol. 1997 Jun;70 (Pt 2):113-47.

[58] Terrizzi, J. A., Jr, & Shook, N. J. (2020). On the Origin of Shame: Does Shame Emerge From an Evolved Disease-Avoidance Architecture? Frontiers in Behavioral Neuroscience, 14.

[59] TenHouten, W. D. (2017). Social dominance hierarchy and the pride–shame system. Journal of Political Power, 10(1), 94–114.

[60] Nathanson D (1997) 'Affect theory and the compass of shame' in Lansky M and Morrison A (eds.) (1997) The widening scope of shame. Hillsdale, NJ: Analytic Press.

[61] Gerodimos, R. (2022). Breaking the cycle of shame and violence: from the individual to the global. In Springer eBooks (pp. 313–334).

[62] Nathanson D (1992) Shame and pride: Affect, sex, and the birth of the self. New York: Norton

[63] Nathanson D (1992) Shame and pride: Affect, sex, and the birth of the self. New York: Norton

[64] Eisikovits, Z., & Enosh, G. (1997). Awareness of guilt and shame in intimate violence. Violence and Victims, 12(4), 307–322.

[65] Chrdileli, M., & Kasser, T. (2018). Guilt, shame, and apologizing behavior: A laboratory study. Personality and Individual Differences, 135, 304–306.

[66] Vaish A. The prosocial functions of early social emotions: the case of guilt. Curr Opin Psychol. 2018 Apr;20:25-29.

[67] Dictionary.com | Meanings & Definitions of English Words. (2024). In Dictionary.com. https://www.dictionary.com/browse/courage

[68] Baumeister, R. F. (2012). Human evil: The myth of pure evil and the true causes of violence. In M. Mikulincer & P. R. Shaver (Eds.), The social psychology of morality: Exploring the causes of good and evil (pp. 367–380). American Psychological Association.

[69] Baumeister, R. F. (2012). Human evil: The myth of pure evil and the true causes of violence. In M. Mikulincer & P. R. Shaver (Eds.), The social psychology of morality: Exploring the causes of good and evil (pp. 367–380). American Psychological Association.

[70] Gendreau P., Goggin C., Cullen F. T., Andrews D. A. (2000). The effects of community sanctions and incarceration on recidivism. Forum on Corrections Research, 12(May), 10-13.

[71] Petrosino, A., Turpin-Petrosino, C., & Buehler, J. (2003). Scared Straight and other juvenile awareness programs for preventing juvenile delinquency: A systematic review of

the randomized experimental evidence. Annals of the American Academy of Political and Social Science, 589, 41–62.

[72] Skiba, R., & Rausch, M. K. (2006). School Disciplinary Systems: Alternatives to Suspension and Expulsion. In G. G. Bear & K. M. Minke (Eds.), Children's needs III: Development, prevention, and intervention (pp. 87–102). National Association of School Psychologists.

[73] Phillips, S., & Maume, M. O. (2007). Have Gun Will Shoot?: Weapon Instrumentality, Intent, and the Violent Escalation of Conflict. Homicide Studies, 11(4), 272-294.

[74] Gendreau P., Goggin C., Cullen F. T., Andrews D. A. (2000). The effects of community sanctions and incarceration on recidivism. Forum on Corrections Research, 12(May), 10-13.

[75] Radelet, M. L., & Lacock, T. L. (2009). Do executions lower homicide rates?: The views of leading criminologists. The Journal of Criminal Law and Criminology (1973-), 99(2), 489–508.

[76] Latimer, J., Dowden, C., & Muise, D. (2005). The Effectiveness of Restorative Justice Practices: A Meta-Analysis. The Prison Journal, 85(2), 127-144. 9

[77] Ward, T., & Maruna, S. (2007). Rehabilitation: Beyond the risk paradigm. Routledge. 6

[78] Scottish Violence Reduction Unit. (2024, May 23). Home - Scottish Violence Reduction Unit. https://www.svru.co.uk/

[79] Violence Prevention (PVL). (2002, October 3). World report on violence and health. https://www.who.int/publications/i/item/9241545615

[80] Violence prevention. (2024, April 9). Violence Prevention. https://www.cdc.gov/violence-prevention/index.html

[81] MSD. (n.d.). Te rito: New Zealand Family Violence Prevention Strategy - Ministry of Social Development. Ministry of Social Development. https://www.msd.govt.nz/about-msd-and-our-work/publications-resources/planning-strategy/te-rito/

[82] Kasser, T. (2002). The High Price of Materialism. MIT Press.

[83] Dittmar, H. (2008). Consumer Culture, Identity and Wellbeing: The Search for the 'Good Life' and the 'Body Perfect'. Psychology Press.

[84] The Australian experience of loneliness. (2022, March 1). Relationships Australia. https://www.relationships.org.au/the-australian-experience-of-loneliness/

[85] Lv M, Zhang M, Huang N, Fu X. Effects of Materialism on Adolescents' Prosocial and Aggressive Behaviors: The Mediating Role of Empathy. Behavioral Sciences. 2023; 13(10):863.

[86] Hardesty, J. L., Ganong, L. H., & Lloyd, S. (Ed.). (2006). How women make custody decisions and manage co-parenting with abusive former husbands. Journal of Social and Personal Relationships, 23(4), 543–563.

[87] Jaffe P et al. 2008. Custody disputes involving allegations of domestic violence: Toward a differentiated approach to parenting plans. Family Court Review 46(3): 500–522

[88] Johnston, J. Roseby, V. & Kuehnle, K. (2009) In the Name of the Child: A developmental approach to understanding and helping children of violent divorce Springer Publishing Company, New York

[89] Kelly, J. B., & Emery, R. E. (2003). Children's adjustment Following divorce: Risk and resilience perspectives. Family Relations, 52(4), 352–362.

[90] Benson, M. L., Fox, G. L., DeMaris, A., & van Wyk, J. (2003). Neighborhood Disadvantage, Individual Economic Distress and Violence Against Women in Intimate Relationships. Journal of Quantitative Criminology, 19(3), 207–235.

[91] Sharp-Jeffs, Nicola (2015) Money Matters : Research into the extent and nature of financial abuse within intimate relationships in the UK. Project Report. London Metropolitan University, London.

[92] Holtzworth-Munroe, A., Bates, L., Smutzler, N., & Sandin, E. (1997). A brief review of the research on husband violence: I. Maritally violent versus nonviolent men. Aggression and Violent Behavior, 2(1), 65–99.

[93] Contact, C. P. A. H. C. a. 2. (2017, December 7). 3. Challenges of current system. https://www.aph.gov.au

[94] Family violence. (n.d.). Attorney-General's Department. https://www.ag.gov.au/families-and-marriage/families/family-violence

[95] Scottish Violence Reduction Unit. (2024, May 23). Home - Scottish Violence Reduction Unit. https://www.svru.co.uk/

[96] Inga Dóra Sigfúsdóttir, Thorolfur Thorlindsson, Álfgeir Logi Kristjánsson, Kathleen M. Roe, John P. Allegrante, Substance use prevention for adolescents: the Icelandic Model, Health Promotion International, Volume 24, Issue 1, March 2009, Pages 16–25.

[97] Campaign for Action on Family Violence, Ministry of Social Development, & Williams, P., Minister of Social Development. (2020). Framework for Change 2019-2023. https://www.msd.govt.nz.

For more titles go to:
www.heart-led.pub/understanding-press

Milton Keynes UK
Ingram Content Group UK Ltd.
UKHW032318121024
449481UK00012B/419